IMPECCABLE RESEARCH

A CONCISE GUIDE TO MASTERING LEGAL RESEARCH SKILLS

Second Edition

■ ■ ■

Mark K. Osbeck
University of Michigan Law School

AMERICAN CASEBOOK SERIES®

WEST
ACADEMIC
PUBLISHING

American Casebook Series is a trademark registered in the U.S. Patent and Trademark Office.

© 2010 Thomson Reuters
© 2016 LEG, Inc. d/b/a West Academic
     444 Cedar Street, Suite 700
     St. Paul, MN 55101
     1-877-888-1330

West, West Academic Publishing, and West Academic are trademarks of West Publishing Corporation, used under license.

Printed in the United States of America

ISBN: 978-0-314-28238-5

To Susan, for planting the seed.

FOREWORD TO THE SECOND EDITION

Electronic research tools have continued to evolve since this book was first published over five years ago—most notably with the introduction of the new electronic research platforms: WestlawNext, Lexis Advance, and Bloomberg Law. But the need for students to follow a sound research strategy has not changed. Accordingly, the heart of the book remains the same in this second edition.

The book has been expanded a bit, however, and it has been updated to reflect these changes in electronic research technology. Thus, the second edition of the book modifies and expands on the first edition in the following ways:

- Chapters 1, 3, 4, and 6 have been modified to reflect the transition to the newer electronic research platforms (i.e., WestlawNext, Lexis Advance, and Bloomberg Law).

- Chapter 7 has been expanded to add an additional section to the Trouble-Shooting Guide on how to find the "best" cases to use.

- Chapters 8 and 9 have been expanded in two ways. First, the discussion of the various primary and secondary sources has been fleshed out, and there is a greater emphasis on free internet sources. Second, there are three additional sections: a new section on *loose-leaf services* in Chapter 8, and new sections on *local law* and on *foreign law/international law* in Chapter 9.

- There is also a new **Research Strategy Checklist** at the end of the book to make it easier for students to assess whether they have properly followed the five-step research strategy set out in Part I of the book.

- Finally, there are some additional, minor changes sprinkled throughout the book to elaborate on certain topics, and to ensure that the material is up to date.

The main purpose of *Impeccable Research* is to provide students a simple, step-by-step guide to the legal research process. I hope you will find this new edition helpful as you continue to hone your skills. Happy research trails!

June 2015

PREFACE

Legal research is an essential part of practicing law. After all, it is through research that lawyers determine what the law is, so that they can counsel clients as to their legal rights. Legal research skills are particularly important for summer associates and newer lawyers because it is they who undertake the lion's share of the legal research burden in most law firms and other employment settings. Therefore, if you are a law student or a beginning lawyer and you want to succeed in the practice of law, you'll need to become a skilled researcher.

While legal research can be fun, it can also be frustrating. Sometimes you easily find precisely what you are looking for; at other times you want to tear your hair out. (Yes, there is a reason why many of us in the profession have thinning hair.) Any lawyer who has practiced law for any length of time knows what it is like to sit in the office late at night, vainly trying to find that one elusive legal authority needed to support a crucial point in an opinion letter or brief that needs to go out the next day. Or what it is like to spend hours researching a complicated legal issue, only to hit a wall and feel like you're no further ahead than when you started. Experiences like this are stressful, and to some extent, they are an inevitable part of legal research. But they can be minimized, and it is the purpose of this book to help you do that.

The central premise of this book is that you need a sound *strategy* for solving your research problems if you are going to be a first-rate researcher. Searching haphazardly for authorities without any clear sense of how a research project should progress from beginning to end is not a recipe for success. The results tend to be hit or miss, and the process inefficient. To be a successful researcher, and to minimize stress, you need to approach research assignments systematically, planning each step in the process, and maintaining a clear focus on your ultimate objective as you proceed with your research. This book can help you do that. It sets out a clear strategy and guides you step-by-step through the research process.

Of course, you don't have to be a law student or a newer lawyer to benefit from this book. Sometimes more senior lawyers can stand to dust off their research skills, particularly if they've been away from research for a while, supervising cases and developing clients.

For lawyers at every level of experience, impeccable research takes careful planning, and it takes discipline. If you adopt a sound strategy for solving legal research problems and follow it faithfully, you will maximize your chances of finding research solutions in an efficient manner. You will also enjoy your research more, and you will likely find fewer opportunities to pull out your hair.

MARK K. OSBECK

ACKNOWLEDGMENTS

Many people have contributed over the years, directly or indirectly, to this project, and I am grateful for all of their contributions. I owe a particular debt of gratitude to my colleagues in the Legal Practice Program at the University of Michigan Law School, who have stimulated my thinking about research strategy and other legal topics in numerous conversations over the years.

I am grateful also to the editorial staff at West Academic Publishing for bringing this book to fruition. Ryan Pfeiffer, in particular, provided invaluable counsel in helping me work through various ideas and in helping me organize the book.

My past and present teaching assistants at the University of Michigan Law School also rendered valuable aid by providing feedback as to the types of research obstacles beginning lawyers are likely to face as they begin their careers. Thanks to J.J. Burns, Bethany Fox, Chris Francis, Danny Grossman, Karen Hinkle, Betsy Martinez, and Gillian Warmflash for their helpful feedback.

I would especially like to thank Danny Grossman, my colleague Paul Falon, and Margaret Leary, Director of the Law Library at the University of Michigan Law School, for their many valuable comments on an earlier draft of the manuscript.

Finally, I would like to thank my mother, Elizabeth Osbeck, for proofreading the manuscript, and I would like to thank my wife, Susan, for both her loving support and her encouragement during this project, and for her wise counsel.

ADDITIONAL ACKNOWLEDGMENTS
FOR THE SECOND EDITION

I am grateful to Patricia Greve and Jesse Medlong for reviewing the manuscript and providing helpful stylistic suggestions. I also wish to thank Howard Bromberg and Ted Becker, my colleagues at the University of Michigan Law School, for their helpful comments and suggestions. I am grateful to various representatives of WestlawNext, Lexis Advance, and Bloomberg Law for providing important information about their products. And I owe special thanks to the editorial staff at West Academic Publishing, in particular Louis Higgins and Mac Soto, for their helpful assistance with this Second Edition.

ABOUT THE AUTHOR

Mark K. Osbeck is a Clinical Professor of Law at the University of Michigan Law School, where he teaches legal research and other experiential skills in the Law School's Legal Practice Program. Prior to joining the faculty at Michigan, Professor Osbeck was an attorney in private practice, first in Washington, D.C., and then in Denver, Colorado, where he was a shareholder with a large law firm.

SUMMARY OF CONTENTS

FOREWORD TO THE SECOND EDITION V

PREFACE VII

ACKNOWLEDGMENTS IX

ABOUT THE AUTHOR XI

Introduction.. 1

PART I. A FIVE-STEP STRATEGY FOR IMPECCABLE LEGAL RESEARCH

Chapter 1. STEP 1: Plan Your Research............... 5
A. Formulating a Research Plan............................... 6
B. Generating Initial Search Terms and Electronic Word-Searches 12

Chapter 2. STEP 2: Consult Secondary Sources 23
A. Using Secondary Sources to Obtain Background Information 25
B. Using Secondary Sources to Refine Your Search Terms.. 28
C. Using Secondary Sources to Find Primary Authorities 29
D. Using Secondary Sources as Persuasive Authorities 31
E. Using Secondary Sources to Re-focus Your Research 33

Chapter 3. STEP 3: Conduct Your Search for Primary Authorities 35
A. Preparing Your Preliminary Outline.................... 36
B. Choosing and Prioritizing Among Primary Sources 38

C. Researching Primary Authorities Within the
    Primary Sources.. 40

**Chapter 4. STEP 4: Expand and Update Your
Case Research** **61**
A. Examining Your Cases for References to Earlier
    Relevant Cases... 62
B. Using Key Numbers to Find Additional Relevant
    Cases 63
C. Using a Citator to Update and Validate Your
    Case Research.. 65
D. Expanding and Updating Your Research for Other
    Types of Primary Authorities.............................. 68

**Chapter 5. STEP 5: Analyze and Organize Your
Research Results** **69**
A. Analyzing Your Research Results........................ 70
B. Organizing Your Research Results 79

**PART II. REFINING YOUR LEGAL
RESEARCH SKILLS**

**Chapter 6. Ten Tips for the Summer Associate
and the Beginning Lawyer** **83**
A. Carry a Legal Pad.. 84
B. Keep the Lines of Communication Open 85
C. Don't Forget: Money Matters 87
D. Learn Your Way Around the Law Library 92
E. Keep Track of Where You've Been and Know
    Where You're Going.. 95
F. Don't Reinvent the Wheel.................................... 96
G. Remember That Annotations and Headnotes Are
    Not Cases 98
H. Find Answers, Not Just Authorities 99
I.   If at First You Don't Succeed, Persist!................ 100
J.   Don't Ignore Those Red Flags! 103

Chapter 7. Trouble-Shooting Guide................... **105**
A. "I'm Not Sure How to Get Started on My
  Research Project." 106
B. "I Don't Know Whether I Should Research a
  Given Project in the Library or Online.".............. 108
C. "I Don't Know How Much Time I Should Devote
  to a Given Project." 111
D. "I'm Not Finding Any Authorities on Point.".......113
E. "My Electronic Word-Searches Are Yielding Too
  Many Cases to Sort Through Efficiently.".......... 117
F. "I'm Half-Way Through My Research Project
  and I'm Really Starting to Feel Confused.".........119
G. "I'm Not Confident in How to Use Persuasive
  Authorities.".. 121
H. "I'm Not Sure When or How I Should End My
  Research.".. 128
I. "I'm Afraid That I Might Have Missed an
  Important Authority.".................................. 130
J. "I Don't Know How to Organize the Results of
  My Research for My Final Work Product.".......... 132
K. "I Don't Know Which Cases Are the 'Best'
  Cases to Use."... 133

PART III. THE PRINCIPAL SOURCES OF LAW—AN OVERVIEW

Chapter 8. Secondary Sources of Law **137**
A. Legal Encyclopedias............................. 138
B. Treatises and Practice Manuals...................... 140
C. Legal Periodicals................................. 142
D. A.L.R.'s 145
E. Restatements of the Law 146
F. Loose-Leaf Services............................. 148
G. Other Secondary Sources 150
H. Digests and Citators 155

Chapter 9. Primary Sources of Law **163**
A. Constitutions.................................. 164

B. Statutes 166
C. Sources of Legislative History 170
D. Regulations 174
E. Cases 179
F. Court Rules 182
G. Local Law 184
H. Foreign Law and International Law 186
I. Other Primary Authorities 191

Research Strategy Checklist **195**

INDEX 199

TABLE OF CONTENTS

FOREWORD TO THE SECOND EDITION.............................. V

PREFACE VII

ACKNOWLEDGMENTS IX

ABOUT THE AUTHOR XI

Introduction.. 1

PART I. A FIVE-STEP STRATEGY FOR IMPECCABLE LEGAL RESEARCH

Chapter 1. STEP 1: Plan Your Research.............. 5
A. Formulating a Research Plan............................. 6
B. Generating Initial Search Terms and Electronic Word-Searches 12
    1. Generating Initial Search Terms.................... 12
    2. Generating Electronic Word-Searches 15

Chapter 2. STEP 2: Consult Secondary Sources 23
A. Using Secondary Sources to Obtain Background Information 25
B. Using Secondary Sources to Refine Your Search Terms.. 28
C. Using Secondary Sources to Find Primary Authorities 29
D. Using Secondary Sources as Persuasive Authorities 31
E. Using Secondary Sources to Re-focus Your Research 33

Chapter 3. STEP 3: Conduct Your Search for Primary Authorities 35
A. Preparing Your Preliminary Outline................... 36

B. Choosing and Prioritizing Among Primary
   Sources 38
C. Researching Primary Authorities Within the
   Primary Sources.. 40
   1. Statutory Research...................................... 40
   2. Regulatory Research 47
   3. Case-Law Research 51
   4. Researching Other Types of Primary
      Authorities... 55

**Chapter 4. STEP 4: Expand and Update Your
Case Research** **61**
A. Examining Your Cases for References to Earlier
   Relevant Cases.. 62
B. Using Key Numbers to Find Additional Relevant
   Cases 63
C. Using a Citator to Update and Validate Your
   Case Research 65
D. Expanding and Updating Your Research for
   Other Types of Primary Authorities 68

**Chapter 5. STEP 5: Analyze and Organize Your
Research Results** **69**
A. Analyzing Your Research Results........................ 70
   1. Pruning Tangential Authorities 70
   2. Prioritizing and Harmonizing Cases.............. 71
      (a) Prioritizing Cases.................................... 72
      (b) Harmonizing Cases.................................. 73
   3. Evaluating Your Answer.............................. 77
B. Organizing Your Research Results 79

PART II. REFINING YOUR LEGAL
RESEARCH SKILLS

**Chapter 6. Ten Tips for the Summer Associate
and the Beginning Lawyer** **83**
A. Carry a Legal Pad.. 84
B. Keep the Lines of Communication Open 85

C. Don't Forget: Money Matters 87
D. Learn Your Way Around the Law Library 92
E. Keep Track of Where You've Been and Know
   Where You're Going 95
F. Don't Reinvent the Wheel 96
G. Remember That Annotations and Headnotes
   Are Not Cases 98
H. Find Answers, Not Just Authorities 99
I. If at First You Don't Succeed, Persist! 100
J. Don't Ignore Those Red Flags! 103

Chapter 7. Trouble-Shooting Guide **105**
A. "I'm Not Sure How to Get Started on My
   Research Project." 106
B. "I Don't Know Whether I Should Research a
   Given Project in the Library or Online." 108
C. "I Don't Know How Much Time I Should Devote
   to a Given Project." 111
D. "I'm Not Finding Any Authorities on Point." 113
E. "My Electronic Word-Searches Are Yielding Too
   Many Cases to Sort Through Efficiently." 117
F. "I'm Half-Way Through My Research Project and
   I'm Really Starting to Feel Confused." 119
G. "I'm Not Confident in How to Use Persuasive
   Authorities." 121
   1. When to Use Persuasive Authorities 122
   2. Which Persuasive Authorities to Use 123
   3. How to Find Persuasive Cases 127
H. "I'm Not Sure When or How I Should End My
   Research." 128
I. "I'm Afraid That I Might Have Missed an
   Important Authority." 130
J. "I Don't Know How to Organize the Results of
   My Research for My Final Work Product." 132
K. "I Don't Know Which Cases Are the 'Best' Cases
   to Use." 133

PART III. THE PRINCIPAL SOURCES OF LAW—AN OVERVIEW

Chapter 8. Secondary Sources of Law **137**
A. Legal Encyclopedias.............................. 138
B. Treatises and Practice Manuals....................... 140
C. Legal Periodicals................................ 142
D. A.L.R.'s 145
E. Restatements of the Law 146
F. Loose-Leaf Services............................ 148
G. Other Secondary Sources 150
H. Digests and Citators 155
    1. Digests 155
    2. Citators 158

Chapter 9. Primary Sources of Law **163**
A. Constitutions.................................. 164
B. Statutes 166
C. Sources of Legislative History........................ 170
D. Regulations 174
E. Cases 179
F. Court Rules 182
G. Local Law 184
H. Foreign Law and International Law.................... 186
    1. Foreign Law.............................. 186
    2. International Law 188
I. Other Primary Authorities....................... 191

Research Strategy Checklist.......................... **195**

INDEX.. 199

IMPECCABLE RESEARCH

A CONCISE GUIDE TO MASTERING LEGAL RESEARCH SKILLS

Second Edition

INTRODUCTION

∎ ∎ ∎

This book is a primer on legal research *strategy*. It presents a systematic, step-by-step approach to solving legal research problems that guides the researcher through each stage of a research project. By consistently following this approach, you can significantly improve the efficiency and accuracy of your research.

I have taught legal research to law students for a number of years, and I have practiced law even longer. Yet I am continually surprised by the number of law students and beginning lawyers who lack a coherent strategy for solving legal research problems. While most are reasonably adept at researching within individual legal sources, such as treatises, cases and statutes, they lack a clear understanding as to the specific steps they should follow when they attempt to find answers to real-world research problems. As a result, most tend to go straight to electronic word-searches to look for cases. They experiment with a variety of hastily devised searches until they eventually stumble upon an authority that appears to be relevant. But then they are unsure about what to do next to expand and update their initial research, and how to complete the project.

The starting point for effective legal research, therefore, is this: divest yourself of the notion that legal research involves nothing more than plugging a few key words into an electronic database to search for cases or other authorities. That approach may work well on Google or Yahoo when you are searching for general information. But it will not generate first-rate legal research. To rely on hastily devised searches at the expense of a more thorough and strategic approach to legal research is to do yourself and your client a disservice.

The purpose of this book is to help you develop a more comprehensive approach to legal research. Part I sets out a systematic, five-step strategy that guides you from the initial framing of your question(s) presented through the final organization of your research results. Part II offers additional guidance to help summer associates and interns develop their research skills in the workplace, and it discusses solutions to some common problems beginning researchers are likely to encounter. And Part III provides an overview of the principal primary and secondary sources of law that you are likely to rely on in your research.

PART I

A FIVE-STEP STRATEGY FOR IMPECCABLE LEGAL RESEARCH

■ ■ ■

Effective legal research requires planning and discipline. It is not an efficient use of your time or your client's money to research haphazardly, without a clear understanding of the specific steps you should take to go about solving the problem. You need to know how to begin a project, how to end it, and what to do in between.

Most legal research texts focus primarily on learning how to work with the various sources of law—that is, how to find and use cases, statutes, regulations, etc. While this is certainly important, it is equally important to have a sound *strategy* to guide you through each step of your research problem.

Imagine that you are learning to play golf. It is one thing to practice your swing at the driving range, learning how to use each of the clubs in your bag. It is quite another to go out on a golf course for the first time and try to negotiate your way from the tees to the holes in an efficient manner. For that you need to know not only *how* to use each club, but also *when* to use each club. You need to know, for example, when you should tee off with an iron rather than a driver, when you should hit with a fairway wood rather than an iron on your second shot, and when you should use your pitching wedge rather than a nine-iron as you approach the green. You need to know a variety of subtler things as well, such as whether you should adjust your club selection when you are hitting into the wind, whether you should try to place the ball short of a stream that

3

intersects the fairway rather than trying to drive over it, and whether you should try to hit the ball long through a group of trees when you are in the rough, or merely plunk it back onto the fairway. In short, you need a basic *strategy* for getting the ball in the hole efficiently— something that goes beyond merely knowing how to use each individual club. You need to know, in other words, how to play golf, not merely how to swing the clubs. And without such knowledge, even a professional-level mastery of each individual club won't make you a great golfer.

The same is true of legal research. Merely learning how to work with individual sources of law to find cases, statutes, regulations, etc., will not make you a first-rate researcher. You also need to know what specific steps to take and when to take them if you are going to solve legal research problems accurately and efficiently. You need, in other words, a sound research *strategy* to guide you through the various stages of research. That is the difference between actually practicing law and merely knowing how to research within the individual sources of law. And only when you master a sound research strategy will you be fully equipped to handle the types of research problems you are likely to encounter in the real-world practice of law.

Part I of this book (Chapters 1–5) lays out a systematic, five-step strategy for solving legal research problems that guides you through each stage of a research project. You can use the **Research Strategy Checklist** at the end of the book to ensure that you have properly followed it.

CHAPTER 1

STEP 1: PLAN YOUR RESEARCH

■ ■ ■

A. Formulating a Research Plan

B. Generating Initial Search Terms and Electronic Word-Searches

    1. Generating Initial Search Terms

    2. Generating Electronic Word-Searches

Suppose it's your first day on a new job as a summer associate. A senior partner has called you in and asked you to help with a research problem. Where do you begin? Unfortunately, for many beginning researchers, the preferred method is to start by running electronic word-searches, using as search terms the first relevant words that come to mind. Then they set about reviewing a mass of responsive cases, many of which have little or no bearing on the actual assignment. And when these beginning researchers finally do find something roughly on point, they do not know what they should do next. They may not even have a clear idea as to what exactly they are supposed to find.

Fortunately, there is a better way. By taking a little time to think through and plan your research before you begin, you can significantly improve the quality and efficiency of your research. Specifically, you need to take a step back and complete two preliminary tasks before you begin to look for legal sources. First, you should think about your research problem carefully and formulate a *research plan* to guide your research. And second, you should generate *search terms* and *electronic word-searches* that are strategically designed to yield answers to your research problem. Undertaking these two advance-planning tasks at the beginning of your research will serve you well later on.

A. FORMULATING A RESEARCH PLAN

The first thing you should do when you begin a research project is formulate a **research plan**. Most importantly, you need to take time to carefully think through the precise question(s) you need to answer (i.e., your **question(s) presented**), and then you need to think about how you are going to find the answers. For many projects, you can just brainstorm for a few minutes and then jot down your question presented, along with the principal issue(s) you plan to address, and the sources of law that you intend to consult to find the answer. But for more complex projects, your research plan should be a little more elaborate, particularly if you are a relatively inexperienced researcher. You might, for example, list several secondary sources to consult and specify the order in which you plan to consult them. You might also want to specify how you intend to search for relevant primary authorities. (For more on finding primary authorities, *see* Chapter 3, section C.) You may also want to expand your research plan by breaking down the question presented into several sub-parts, and then noting with respect to each sub-part the issues you need to address and the sources of law you plan to consult in researching them.

How elaborate and how formal your research plan is will depend upon the complexity of your project, as well as on your comfort level and knowledge of the subject matter, your level of experience, and the time constraints you face. But the important point is that you shouldn't start looking for legal authorities without first analyzing carefully the precise question(s) you are trying to answer, and how it differs from related questions that are not at issue. After that, you should consider which sources you intend to consult to find the answer.

Consider, for example, the following research assignment. Suppose you have been asked to research whether the contract doctrine of *illegality* applies when a contract is *performed* in an illegal manner, even though it was not entered into for an illegal *purpose*. Specifically, your client entered into an agreement with a friend to form a partnership. The purpose of the partnership agreement was legitimate: to form a business that would install network systems. Later, in the course of running the business, both partners engaged in a number of illegal activities, such as bribing public officials to obtain work. Now your client is suing his former partner for breach of the partnership agreement for failing to pay your client his share of the partnership's profits. The former partner's defense is that the partnership agreement is void under the contract doctrine of *illegality*. (Simply stated, the doctrine of illegality holds that courts will refuse to enforce illegal contracts, e.g., a contract to kill someone, as a matter of public policy; in these instances, the contract, as a matter of law, is deemed to be void.) Your assignment is to figure out whether the defendant's illegality defense is likely to succeed, given that the parties entered the agreement for a legitimate purpose, and that the illegal acts occurred only later in the performance of the contract.

To solve this problem, you'll first want to formulate a research plan. Start by thinking carefully through the question presented. Generally, in formulating the question presented, you'll want to think in terms of abstract *concepts*, such as the relationship between the parties (e.g., a partnership), the *legal issues* involved (e.g., under what circumstances the illegality doctrine applies), the *relief sought* (e.g., enforcement of the contract) and any possible *defenses* to enforcement. Your question presented should also incorporate any key *facts* that you think are important to the analysis, and it should reference the controlling *jurisdiction*. While there is no one correct way to frame a question presented, it is important that you think through exactly what it is you need to figure out (and write it down), so that you don't start researching with just a vague idea as to the question you are trying to answer. Otherwise, the answer you find may turn out to be only tangentially relevant to your question presented.

A broad way to frame the principal question presented by the illegality hypothetical would be as follows: *Under what circumstances does the illegality defense apply in an action for enforcement of an agreement?* A more precise formulation that includes the parties' relationship (i.e., as partners) and the jurisdiction might be: *Under North Carolina law, does the illegality doctrine apply when a partnership agreement was performed in an illegal manner, but the parties' purpose in entering the agreement was legitimate?* Or you might focus in even more precisely by framing the question like this: *Under North Carolina law, does the illegality defense prevent a court from enforcing a partnership agreement, where the partnership was not created for an illegal purpose, but the partners later engaged in illegal acts in performing the business affairs of the partnership?*

Having formulated your question presented, you should then give some thought to the principal issues it raises. Does it matter, for example, that the illegality pertained only to the parties' actions in *performing* the agreement and not to the *purpose* for which the agreement was entered? Does it matter how many illegal actions were performed? Does it matter that both parties committed illegal actions, rather than just the party seeking damages? The answers to these questions may well determine your ultimate answer.

Once you are clear on the question(s) presented by your research, and the principal issues it raises, the final task in formulating a research plan is deciding what *legal sources* you want to consult, and in what order. This will depend to some extent upon your familiarity with the area of law, and it will also depend upon certain external considerations, such as your time constraints. Normally, however, you will want to start by reviewing one or more *secondary sources*, in order to gain a general understanding of the problem and to give you a head start on locating primary authorities. (*See* Chapter 2, sections A, B, and C, for more on using secondary sources to start your research.) Then you will want to turn your attention to finding controlling *primary authorities* (e.g., statutes or cases), starting with the source of law that you think is most fundamental for this particular problem. (*See* Chapter 3, section B, for more on choosing among primary sources.) And if you cannot find any controlling authorities on point, you may then want to search for some *persuasive authorities*. (For additional information on persuasive authorities, *see* Chapter 7, section G.)

With respect to the illegality problem discussed above, for example, my tentative plan would be as follows:

- First, I would start with a broad *secondary source* (**Step 2**), such as a contracts treatise, or perhaps an A.L.R. article, in order to learn the basic parameters of the illegality doctrine and to get some references to key primary authorities. (For background on the various types of secondary sources available and their uses, *see* Chapter 8.)

- Next, I would plan to look for *primary authorities* in the controlling jurisdiction (**Step 3**). Since we know from the first year of law school that contract law (outside of the area of government contracts) is principally based upon state law rather than federal law, and upon decisional law rather than legislation, I would first look for relevant *state cases* from North Carolina.

- Then I would do a quick search for any relevant *state statutes*, just to make sure the legislature in the controlling jurisdiction (North Carolina) had not altered the common-law doctrine.

- If my search for relevant cases in the controlling jurisdiction did not fully address the problem, I would then look for *persuasive cases* that were more on point (i.e., federal cases from North Carolina and appellate cases from other states).

• Lastly, I would *expand and update* my case research (**Step 4**), before subjecting it to a *final analysis and organization* (**Step 5**).

I would alter this plan a little on the fly if, after reviewing secondary sources in **Step 2**, I learned that one of my initial assumptions was incorrect (if I learned, for example, that there is in fact a statute that governs the analysis in the controlling jurisdiction). But this initial research plan would nevertheless provide me with a solid foundation for conducting my search for authorities.

Keeping good records as you proceed with your research is important. At a minimum, you'll want to memorialize your research trail (i.e., your searches and the authorities they led you to), and you'll want to "link" each authority you deem important to the point(s) in your preliminary outline that it supports. (For more on preparing a preliminary outline, *see* Chapter 3, section A.) It is also a good idea to keep copies of the important authorities you find.

The principal online commercial services (i.e. WestlawNext, Lexis Advance, and Bloomberg Law) can be very helpful with regard to record-keeping. They automatically track your research trail (*see, e.g.,* the *History* tab on WestlawNext), and they make available electronic "folders" in which you can store copies of any important authorities you find as you proceed with your research. (For more on the importance of keeping good records as you research, *see* Chapter 6, sections A and E.)

Whether it is complex or simple, formulating a research plan is important, particularly for less-experienced researchers, because it provides direction for your research. It clarifies your ultimate objective (i.e., the precise legal research problem you need to solve), and it provides a roadmap to help you get there.

B. GENERATING INITIAL SEARCH TERMS AND ELECTRONIC WORD-SEARCHES

In addition to developing a research plan, you should also give some thought to generating effective **search terms** before you begin your actual research. And if you plan to use full-text searches online, you will also want to formulate some initial **electronic word-searches**. *Search terms* are individual words or phrases that are used to access indexes and tables of contents for the various sources of law; *electronic word-searches* are combinations of search terms arranged in such a way that they enable full-text searches of documents. The success of your research project will hinge in no small measure on how skillfully you employ these linguistic tools.

1. GENERATING INITIAL SEARCH TERMS

Whether you are researching online or in a library, you will need to start with basic *search terms* in order to efficiently and accurately locate legal authorities. These terms enable you to access indexes and tables of contents for various authorities, and they also serve as the building blocks for your electronic word-searches if you decide to run full-text searches online. Generally, if you've adequately framed your question presented, and made a list of the principal legal issues it raises, your search terms should flow naturally from these formulations. You may, however, have to supplement the terms or modify them to ensure that they are not too broad or narrow.

Suppose, for example, you are trying to generate search terms to research the contract-illegality problem discussed in section A of this chapter. And suppose you prepared the following question presented:

Under North Carolina law, does the illegality defense prevent a court from enforcing a partnership agreement, where the partnership was not created for an illegal purpose, but the partners later engaged in illegal acts in performing the business affairs of the partnership?

You could start by generating some simple search terms, such as "partnership," "agreement," "illegality," "illegality defense," "illegal acts," "enforce," and "purpose," that flow directly from the wording of the question presented. These terms would likely be sufficient to enable you to find relevant entries in the topical index or table of contents of a particular source, such as a treatise or a digest.

But they might miss some relevant entries if you don't broaden them a bit. For one thing, you would need to consider different *variations* of the key words. You may, for example, find a discussion of illegality listed under an index heading such as *Illegal Bargains* rather than the heading *Illegality Defense*. Likewise, you might find a discussion of specific performance under a heading such as *Contractual Remedies* (or just *Remedies*) rather than under the headings *Contracts*. So it is important to be flexible and consider variations of your search terms. It is also important to consider *synonyms* for your search terms. If, for example, you are looking at the index to a secondary source for entries under the heading *Contracts*, you'll also want to look under the heading *Agreements*. Likewise, if you are searching the index to a digest for cases concerning overdrawn checks, you'll want to look for the heading *Drafts* in addition to the heading *Checks*.

But even if you employ synonyms that properly capture word variations, your initial search terms may still prove to be too narrow if you fail to think *conceptually* about the answers you are looking for. The Restatement (Second) of Contracts, for example, does not discuss the illegality doctrine *per se*, but instead includes a discussion about the enforcement of contracts entered into for an illegal purpose under a more general chapter entitled *Unenforceability on Grounds of Public Policy*. (*See* Restatement (Second) of Contracts § 178, *et seq.* (1979)). You would therefore need to think more broadly about the various *categories* of contract defenses, rather than just the particular defense of illegality, in order to find the Restatement's discussion about the enforceability of illegal contracts.

So if your initial search terms are not productive, it is helpful to think of broader concepts that encompass them. Instead of "checks" or "drafts," for example, try broader categories such as "commercial paper" or "negotiable instruments." Instead of "dogs" and "cats," try "house pets," or "domestic animals." Sometimes it is necessary to think creatively about how the editor might have designated a topic and to try some different possibilities if you don't see what you are looking for right away.

By generating search terms in this way, you should generally be able to locate authorities in most legal sources without too much difficulty, whether you are looking in print sources or online. Most legal sources are thoroughly indexed, so normally you can do all or most of your research without the benefit of electronic word-searches if you choose to do so. Generally, however, as discussed in Chapter 3, it is best to be redundant and use more than one research tool in order to ensure the accuracy of your research.

2. GENERATING ELECTRONIC WORD-SEARCHES

While using the types of individual search terms discussed in the previous section would generally enable you to access tables of contents and indexes effectively, using *electronic word-searches* to find authorities requires a little more finesse. Thus, in addition to generating individual search terms at the beginning of your project, you should also think about how you are going to *combine* these search terms into electronic word-searches, if you plan to do at least some of your research by executing full-text searches of documents. And you should plan on revisiting these searches (*see* Chapter 2, section B) after you have had a chance to review secondary sources (**Step 2**), because the secondary sources will often provide you with terms of art that you can use for additional search terms.

Electronic word-searches can be very helpful when used properly because they allow you to customize your search efforts. You can use electronic word-searches to focus in on relevant materials with great precision. Thus, in the hands of skilled researchers, electronic word-searches promote efficiency because they allow researchers to find what they are looking for very quickly.

There are basically two types of electronic word-searches that you can run on commercial services such as WestlawNext, Lexis Advance, and Bloomberg Law. The easier type of electronic word-search to use is a *natural-language search (i.e., descriptive term search)*, which is probably what you are familiar with from generic internet searching. (It is also the default option on the commercial services.) With natural-language searches, you just enter a question, a phrase or just a combination of descriptive search terms (e.g., "contract illegal enforcement"), and the search engine does the work for you, listing in descending order (from most relevant to least relevant) a set number of documents that are responsive to your search.

The other type of electronic word-search is a *terms-and-connectors* search (also known as a "Boolean" search), which allows you to specify the precise relationship between the search terms you employ by using logical symbols. For example, you might run an electronic word-search such as "(contract /3 illegal) /s enforce," which instructs the search engine to first find only those authorities that combine the words "contract" and "illegal" within three words of each other, and to then narrow the results to those that also contain that combination within the same sentence as the word "enforce."

If you include connectors such as "/3" in your basic search, the search engine will automatically run a terms-and-connectors search. If your search is comprised of strictly descriptive terms, such as "contract illegal," then the search engine will run it as a natural-language search.

When you formulate search terms for purposes of terms-and-connectors searches, you want to make sure you capture all the other possible variations of the terms (e.g., "contractual" as well as "contract," "illegal" as well as "illegality") so that your search casts a wide enough net. (The newer search engines automatically correct for simple plurals.) The newer search engines (e.g., WestlawNext) do a better job of capturing variations than the older versions (e.g., Classic Westlaw) did. But to be safe, it's still best to add the exclamation point symbol ["!"] to the root of a word, which enables the search to capture all possible variations of the root. For example, by using "enforc!" as a search term, you can capture all the different variations of the root, such as "enforce," "enforcement," "enforceable," and "enforcing." And if you just want to capture simple, one-character variations (e.g., "men" as well as "man"), you can instead add an asterisk symbol [*] to a word, which enables the search to capture one wildcard character. Remember also that you'll need to account for synonyms in terms-and-connectors searches (*e.g.,* "contracts"/ "agreements"), just as you do when consulting an index.

Crafting effective terms-and-connectors searches can be challenging, as there is no simple algorithm for how to combine search terms and connectors into electronic word-searches. One technique that is helpful, though, is to think about the type of legal *rule* you are looking for with your search, and to anticipate how the courts or legislature would likely have worded such a rule. Then you can use terms and connectors to frame your search so that it captures cases with the same or related wording. With the illegality hypothetical, for example, you might anticipate finding a rule in the case law to the effect that *contracts formed for an illegal purpose are not enforceable.* To capture cases following such a rule, you could frame a terms-and-connectors search such as: *"contract* or agreement /s "illegal purpose" /s enforc!".* Formulating the search in this way would enable the search engine to find cases that track the wording of your anticipated rule. (You should be prepared to broaden your initial search as described below, however, if it does not yield as many cases on point as you anticipated.)

Ideally, of course, the goal is to formulate your electronic word-searches in such a way that you find *all* the relevant authorities that are out there and *only* those relevant authorities. Unfortunately, in the real world, that is not generally going to happen. But you want to do your best to make your electronic word-searches *broad* enough so that you don't miss important authorities, and *narrow* enough that you don't waste a lot of time reviewing irrelevant authorities. And it is finding the proper balance between overly broad and overly narrow that makes crafting effective electronic word-searches challenging for the legal researcher. As a general rule, however, it is a good idea to err on the side of broadness in your initial searches so that you don't miss important authorities; you can easily edit your search to make it narrower if the initial search turns out to be too broad.

One way to *broaden* electronic word-searches is to use more expansive search terms, as discussed in the previous section. Additionally, you can broaden the scope of your searches by using *fewer* search terms. A search like "contract illegality," for example, will normally generate more responsive hits than a search like "contract illegality purpose performance." And if you are using *terms-and-connectors* searches, you can make your searches broader by using less restrictive connectors. Replacing the connector "/3" with a broader connector such as "/15" or "/p," for example, or replacing an "and" with an "or," will cause your search to cast a wider net.

On the other hand, if you find that your research results are unmanageable because you are generating too many tangentially related responses, you will want to edit your searches to make them *narrower*. To do this, you should first consider whether your database is too broad. If you are running searches for Ohio cases on illegality using an *all-state-cases* database, for example, you'll do better with a more restrictive database containing only Ohio cases. Using more narrowly crafted search terms that track the facts of your research problem can also help you search with greater precision. For example, if "negotiable instrument" proves to be too broad a term, try "draft" instead, if in fact that is the type of negotiable instrument that your client received from the defendant. If "chattel" yields too many results, try "engagement ring," if that is the type of chattel your client is trying to recover from his former fiancée.

Another way to narrow your electronic word-searches is to add additional search terms. With the illegality problem, for example, you may capture too many irrelevant cases if you just use a broad, natural-language word search such as "contract illegal." You can limit the search to cases that discuss the distinction between contracts formed for an illegal *purpose* and those that involve illegality in the *performance* of the contract by adding those terms to your search. The search engines also allow you to exclude certain superfluous terms in a natural-language search, and to make others mandatory.

If you are using terms-and-connectors searches, you can also narrow your electronic word-searches by using more restrictive *connectors*. For example, you can use an "/s" instead of a "/p," an "and" instead of an "or," and a "/5" instead of a "/10." The online commercial services also give you the option of restricting the *search field* (or *segment* as Lexis calls it), so that you can confine your search to cases arising from a particular court, to those written by a particular judge, to those decided after a particular date, etc. One good way to narrow a search when you get too many results is to use the "synopsis" and "digest" fields. This ensures that the search terms you use appear both in the headnotes of the case and in the editor's summary of the case's holding, which means that the terms are likely to be central to the court's holding.

Setting off certain operations with parentheses is another useful tool for narrowing searches. This tells the search engine to perform that operation first before executing the rest of the search. Similarly, setting off key terms with quotation marks (e.g., "illegal contract") tells the search engine to read the terms as a phrase rather than as separate search terms.

Beginning researchers often wonder whether it is better to use natural-language searches or terms-and-connectors searches in their research. Unfortunately, there is no simple answer to this question, and to a large extent, the choice between the two types of searches depends upon personal preference. However, I generally suggest that students begin typical research projects with natural-language searches, and employ terms-and-connectors searches only if they are having a difficult time finding precisely what they're looking for. Terms-and-connectors searches offer greater precision, but they are also less forgiving than natural-language searches. Novice researchers, in particular, may miss the mark when using terms-and-connectors searches because they don't formulate them quite right.

Terms-and-connectors searches do have advantages, however, in certain contexts where precision is key. Thus, if you're looking for a particular term of art or a particular document, or if you are looking for specific information, such as all cases that mention a certain company, then terms-and-connectors searches are likely to be more accurate. But I don't recommend that beginning researchers rely on them for the bulk of their searches.

If you do decide to run a terms-and-connectors search, and you are not too familiar with formulating such searches, the search engines offer some assistance. WestlawNext, for example, has an "Advanced Search" feature that is helpful. Just click on the small "advanced" link next to the *Search* tab, and the program will help you construct a terms-and-connectors search from your descriptive terms. This feature is also helpful if you want to narrow your search by "fields," such as the synopsis/digest fields discussed above. Lexis Advance has a similar function, also called "Advanced Search," which you can access via the *Filters* tab.

The principal online commercial services (i.e., WestlawNext, Lexis Advance, and Bloomberg Law) also provide online tutorials that can help you sharpen your skills in crafting electronic-word searches. Furthermore, these services provide phone and e-mail access to research attorneys who are adept at formulating electronic word-searches, should you encounter problems with your research.

It is important to remain flexible when crafting your searches. In spite of your best efforts, your initial searches will sometimes be too broad or too narrow. Thus, you will need to be prepared to modify them and try new terms and combinations of terms (and connectors) as you proceed with your research. Few researchers are so proficient that they always, or even usually, find all and only the most relevant authorities with their initial search. So don't be discouraged— persistence is one of the most important qualities of effective researchers (*see* Chapter 6, section I).

But remember, it is important to spend some time at the beginning of your research project thinking about effective search terms and how to combine them into electronic word-searches. This small investment of time will pay handsome dividends as your research proceeds through the next four research steps discussed below.

CHAPTER 2

STEP 2: CONSULT SECONDARY SOURCES

■ ■ ■

A. Using Secondary Sources to Obtain Background Information

B. Using Secondary Sources to Refine Your Search Terms

C. Using Secondary Sources to Find Primary Authorities

D. Using Secondary Sources as Persuasive Authorities

E. Using Secondary Sources to Re-focus Your Research

One common mistake law students and beginning lawyers make when researching is failing to take full advantage of *secondary sources*. Secondary sources are materials such as treatises, legal encyclopedias, law-review articles, etc., that contain information and commentary *about* legal authorities, as opposed to the legal authorities themselves. (For more information about the individual secondary sources mentioned in this chapter, *see* Chapter 8.) Many law students and beginning lawyers see researching secondary sources as a superfluous step that they can circumvent by going directly to primary sources via electronic word-searches. But in doing so, they ignore a valuable resource.

To be sure, there are times when an experienced researcher who knows a good deal about an area of law may elect to skip this step, particularly when facing a serious time constraint, or when all that is needed is a quick search for an authority to support a point of law. But skipping this step as a beginning researcher is ill-advised because you generally lack adequate familiarity with the subject matter to put your research results in context. Secondary sources are a rich and valuable source of information. By making proper use of them, you lower your risk of missing important authorities, and you also increase the efficiency of your research because you are not trying to reinvent the wheel looking for information that has already been compiled.

As discussed below, secondary sources are valuable in five principal ways: (1) they can provide helpful background information about a problem and frame it in its proper context; (2) they can help you refine your initial search terms and your electronic word-searches; (3) they can provide a head start on finding *primary authorities*; (4) they can themselves serve as *persuasive authorities*; and (5) they can help you re-focus your thinking and get your research back on track when your initial searches are not going as planned. So you should take full advantage of secondary sources for each of these purposes; your legal research will benefit significantly if you do.

A. USING SECONDARY SOURCES TO OBTAIN BACKGROUND INFORMATION

One of the principal uses of secondary sources is to provide background information on a research topic. This is important because it gives you an understanding of how your research fits into a larger context, which in turn focuses your research and keeps it on track.

Suppose, for example, that you have received the following assignment. Your employer represents a client in federal court. The other side has moved for summary judgment. Your opponent's motion for summary judgment is supported by an affidavit that contains numerous allegations about what some third party witness has stated. Your supervisor wants to file a motion asking the court to strike the affidavit because it is based on inadmissible evidence. She has asked you to research whether an affidavit offered in support of a motion for summary judgment in federal court can be stricken if it is based on an out-of-court statement by a third party.

Now if you know a fair amount about civil procedure and evidence, you might be able to find the answer efficiently by first reviewing Federal Rule of Civil Procedure 56, and in particular section (c)(4), which tells us, among other things, that the affidavit "must be made on personal knowledge, set out facts that would be *admissible in evidence,* and show that the affiant or declarant is competent to testify on the matters stated." (emphasis added) You could then look to the controlling cases to see what they say about the admissibility of out-of-court statements. But if you are not especially conversant with the Federal Rules of Civil Procedure and the Federal Rules of Evidence, you will probably benefit from obtaining some background information on the law before you begin your search for cases interpreting Rule 56. And depending on your level of knowledge, you may need more or less background information.

If you are not a litigator, you may need a brief primer on the hearsay rule and its exceptions before you begin to look for primary authorities. Some out-of-court statements that look at first blush like hearsay do not actually constitute hearsay under Rule 801 of the Federal Rules of Evidence, and other statements that do constitute hearsay are nevertheless exempted from the prohibition of the hearsay rule and allowed into evidence if they meet one of the hearsay exceptions set out in Rules 803 and 804. So in order to really understand cases interpreting Rule 56(c), you need to know a little something about hearsay statements and their admissibility.

Where would you look for a background discussion on hearsay? Well, you have a number of options. You could consult one of the general legal encyclopedias: *Corpus Juris Secundum ("C.J.S.")* or *American Jurisprudence, Second Edition ("Am. Jur. 2d")*. There you could quickly locate a cursory discussion on the hearsay rule, either by perusing the general index for "Hearsay" or by examining the table of contents under the topic of "Evidence." For a more in-depth discussion, you could take a look at a multi-volume treatise on evidence, such as *McCormick on Evidence*, focusing on the chapter(s) on hearsay. Alternatively, you could look under "Hearsay" in the general index to the American Law Reports ("A.L.R.'s") to see if there are any annotations that address your specific topic. Or, if your case is set in state court rather than federal court, you could review a state practice manual; these practical guides are very helpful for getting an overview of state-specific law. The important thing is not so much *which* secondary source you initially consult, but rather *that* you consult one or more in order to gain a basic understanding of the law before plunging into the cases. Whichever secondary source you choose will likely provide you cross-references to other secondary sources on point, so you can easily go from one secondary source to another to gain additional information. (For more on individual secondary sources, *see* Chapter 8.)

With respect to our hypothetical research problem on affidavit requirements, the other secondary research I would want to undertake, before I turned to cases interpreting Rule 56, would be research on the basic concepts of Rule 56 itself. Again, if you are an experienced litigator and you understand the rules of civil procedure quite well, this may not be necessary. But if you do not, then it would be helpful to gain a basic understanding of how the summary judgment procedure set out in Rule 56 works, particularly subsection (c), which deals with the requirements and procedures for supporting or opposing a claim that there is a genuine dispute as to the facts. For this, the best choice is probably one of the classic treatises on the Federal Rules of Civil Procedure: either Wright & Miller's *Federal Practice and Procedure,* or *Moore's Federal Practice.* These multi-volume works contain a wealth of information about the federal rules of evidence and procedure and are easy to access. They discuss the rules in numerical order, so you need merely to turn to the chapter(s) on Rule 56 of the Federal Rules of Civil Procedure and scan the relevant sections for one dealing with Rule 56(c). The information you glean from a quick review of that section will focus your subsequent case research and help to keep you from getting off track on a tangential point.

The other, somewhat hidden, benefit to regularly using secondary sources to acquire background information at the beginning of your research is that, in the long run, the practice makes you not only a better researcher, but also a more knowledgeable lawyer. Why? Because when you try to understand the big picture about the topics you are researching, instead of just finding the answers to the narrow questions you are assigned, over time you begin to weave together an understanding of the law as a whole that continues to grow the longer you practice and the more you learn about individual topics. This 'gestalt' view of the law will serve you well as you transition from a beginning lawyer who researches specific legal problems to a seasoned counselor whose valued advice clients actively seek out.

B. USING SECONDARY SOURCES TO REFINE YOUR SEARCH TERMS

An additional reason to review secondary sources before you begin an independent search for primary authorities is to refine your search terms. You should pay particular attention to the terminology the secondary sources use when they discuss the applicable topic; they frequently contain important terms of art that will be useful in focusing your subsequent searches.

Suppose, once again, that you are researching the admissibility of affidavits that rely on out-of-court, third-party statements. You will likely learn from your review of secondary sources that a major test for whether an affidavit is admissible is whether the information it relies on would be **admissible at trial**. In the case of an out-of-court declaration, this determination largely turns on whether the statement constitutes a **hearsay statement**, and if so, whether the statement comes within one of the **hearsay exceptions** set out in **Rules 803 and 804**. Under **Rule 801**, whether it constitutes hearsay depends on whether it is being used to prove the **truth of the matter asserted**. Thus, by going back to secondary sources and paying close attention to the particular terminology they use, you can often pick up certain key search terms that you might not otherwise have thought of, such as those set off above in boldface, that would likely make your searches more effective.

Or suppose you are researching Florida law on the meaning of the *intent* element under the tort doctrine of *intentional infliction of emotional distress.* By reviewing a state practice manual or state-specific encyclopedia for Florida, you would probably learn right away that an alternative name for intentional infliction of emotional distress in Florida is the tort of *outrage.* By including that term in your searches as a synonym for intentional infliction of emotional distress, you would lessen the risk of missing important authorities on point. But you probably wouldn't know to include **outrage** as a search term if you hadn't reviewed one or more secondary sources.

Thus, in addition to providing background information, a review of appropriate secondary sources can help to sharpen your search terms, thereby making it easier for you to find primary authorities when you move on to **Step 3** of your research.

C. USING SECONDARY SOURCES TO FIND PRIMARY AUTHORITIES

Another important reason for using secondary sources is that they often refer you directly to key *primary authorities.* Thus, in addition to reviewing secondary sources for background information and to refine your search terms, you can use their footnotes to find helpful references to primary authorities. This will give you a head start on **Step 3** of your research, which is discussed in the following chapter.

In recent years, electronic word-searches have tended to push secondary sources into the background somewhat as tools for finding primary authorities. But secondary sources are still very helpful in this regard, especially since certain secondary sources, such as multi-volume treatises, loose-leaf services, A.L.R.'s, and state practice-manuals, will generally identify for you the authorities that are most significant on a given topic within a given jurisdiction.

With respect to the summary judgment problem discussed above, for example, a treatise such as Wright & Miller's *Federal Practice and Procedure* not only provides helpful background information that frames the legal context of Rule 56(c)(4), it also points you to key cases that interpret that rule, including those that deal specifically with affidavits containing hearsay statements. Section 2738 of the treatise, entitled *Affidavits in Support of or in Opposition to Summary Judgment*, provides a helpful discussion of the requirements for affidavits submitted in connection with motions for summary judgment, along with footnotes that contain citations to representative cases. In footnote 17 of this section, there are numerous citations to cases discussing the propriety of affidavits that contain hearsay statements, drawn from a variety of jurisdictions. So whatever jurisdiction your problem is set in, there is a decent chance you will find a case on point in that jurisdiction. And even if you do not, you can easily use West's *Key Number System* to find similar cases in the controlling jurisdiction. (*See* Chapter 4, section B, and Chapter 8, section H(1)), for more about using the West Key Number System.)

Make sure that if you are researching in print versions of secondary sources, you check the *pocket parts* and *supplements* for the latest commentary and cases. While the principal online commercial services (i.e., WestlawNext, Bloomberg Law, and Lexis Advance) will continually update their databases, print sources rely on pocket parts (in the back of each volume) and supplements to keep current. In fact, for some secondary sources, such as the Restatements, the number of supplemental volumes far exceeds the number of original volumes because the cascade of judicial opinions keeps filling more and more supplemental volumes.

D. USING SECONDARY SOURCES AS PERSUASIVE AUTHORITIES

In addition to helping you find primary authorities, secondary sources can themselves serve as *persuasive authorities* in certain situations. Occasionally, when you are researching an issue of law in a jurisdiction whose law is unsettled in that area, you may want to cite a secondary source as persuasive authority to convince the court that your position is the more reasonable or more widely accepted position.

Suppose, for example, that the summary judgment assignment discussed above concerned a lawsuit in state court rather than federal court, and that the decisional law of the controlling state regarding the requirements for affidavits offered in support of motions for summary judgment was rather sparse. Assuming the state's civil procedural rules were roughly comparable to the Federal Rules of Civil Procedure, as they are in most states, you might want to cite to § 2738 of Wright & Miller's *Federal Practice and Procedure* as persuasive authority for your argument that the court should strike your opponent's affidavit pursuant to Rule 56(c)(4) because the affidavit is based on inadmissible hearsay. In the absence of any controlling state law on point, this well-respected treatise provides guidance to the court as to the interpretation other courts have given Rule 56(c)(4), and as to the policy rationale for that interpretation.

Knowing just how to use secondary sources as persuasive authority, however, can be a little tricky. For starters, not all secondary sources have equal weight for this purpose. An A.L.R. annotation, for example, will generally have little persuasive force with the courts, as it is primarily a compilation of case abstracts without independent analysis. Likewise, legal encyclopedias have little persuasive force. On the other hand, citing one of the Restatements, if you are dealing with an area governed primarily by decisional law, or citing a respected, multi-volume treatise, such as *Federal Practice and Procedure,* can be quite persuasive. It is not uncommon for the courts themselves to cite these types of secondary sources in their opinions, either as evidence of a majority rule, or in support of an argument that a certain position is more reasonable. Other types of secondary authorities, such as law-review articles and practice manuals, fall somewhere in-between. While courts seem to cite law-review articles for authority less frequently than they once did, perhaps because these articles as a group have become somewhat less practical over the years, a good law-review article that is precisely on point can still have significant persuasive force. For articles as well as treatises, considerations such as the reputation of the author(s) and whether the work is recent (or recently updated) will significantly affect their persuasiveness.

You should be careful not to over-use secondary sources as persuasive authorities. It makes little sense to cite a secondary source in support of an argument if there is a controlling primary authority on point. And even if there are no controlling primary authorities on point, citing a case from another jurisdiction is often more persuasive than citing a secondary source, particularly if the case is factually on par with your case. Generally, therefore, you want to make conservative use of secondary sources as persuasive authorities, though in the right circumstances they can be useful for this purpose. (For more on using persuasive authorities effectively, *see* Chapter 7, section G.)

E. USING SECONDARY SOURCES TO RE-FOCUS YOUR RESEARCH

Finally, secondary sources can serve as helpful tools for keeping your research focused after you've begun your search for primary authorities. At times, your initial research will be unproductive, or it will take unexpected turns that leave you feeling less sure about the issue you are researching than you were before you started. In such circumstances, revisiting appropriate secondary sources can help to get you back on track and re-orient your research. (For more tips on how to re-focus your research when you are feeling confused, *see* Chapter 7, section F.)

Remember that your research plan is not static: it is merely a starting point, and you will likely need to modify it as you proceed. You cannot always anticipate how your research is going to play out, so you have to be flexible and be prepared to alter your game plan as you go. You may discover after you complete your initial research that the problem is a little different from what you first envisioned, or that your initial assumptions about the law were not quite correct. Or your initial searches may simply turn out to be unproductive. In these circumstances, reviewing an appropriate secondary source can clarify your understanding of the legal context and help you re-formulate your question presented before you proceed further down the wrong path.

Suppose, for example, that your initial search for primary authorities on the requirements for summary-judgment affidavits hit a wall because you didn't adequately review a secondary source on the rules of evidence before you began your search for primary authorities. Instead you relied on the overly simplified assumption that affidavits may not be based on hearsay. Then you found some cases holding that an affidavit may rely on hearsay, as long as the hearsay statement in question falls within one of the hearsay exceptions set out in F.R.E. 803 and 804. At that point, you should go back to a secondary source, such as *McCormick on Evidence*, to brush up on the exceptions to the hearsay rule, so that you can better evaluate whether the affidavit you are concerned with contains admissible evidence.

The principal online commercial services make it easy to go back and forth from primary authorities to secondary sources after you have begun your initial search for primary authorities. They use your search terms to automatically find secondary sources and other useful materials on point whenever you do a search for primary authorities. Thus, if you are researching online and your search for primary authorities is getting off track, you can filter for secondary sources (instead of, say, cases), and then inspect the secondary sources that are automatically generated to see if one of these addresses your issue. You can also look within a particular secondary source for references to other secondary sources that might be helpful.

Remember, legal research sometimes takes unexpected turns, so you should not lose heart merely because your initial research plan did not take you directly to the answer you were seeking. Legal research is difficult, and it requires patience. Trial and error are simply part of the process. But consulting secondary sources, both in the early stages of your research and again later in your research if things don't go quite as planned, can make the process proceed more smoothly.

CHAPTER 3

STEP 3: CONDUCT YOUR
SEARCH FOR PRIMARY AUTHORITIES

■ ■ ■

A. Preparing Your Preliminary Outline

B. Choosing and Prioritizing Among Primary Sources

C. Researching Primary Authorities Within the Primary Sources

1. Statutory Research

2. Regulatory Research

3. Case-Law Research

4. Researching Other Types of Primary Authorities

Once you have taken the foundational steps set out in the previous two chapters of the book, you are ready to look for primary authorities, using the search terms and electronic word-searches you generated in **Step 1** and refined in **Step 2**. First, you will want to prepare a *preliminary outline* of the major issues before you begin your search for primary authorities. Next, you will need to decide which *primary sources* to look at for each issue. And lastly, you will need to find relevant *primary authorities* within those sources. Each of these steps is discussed in turn below.

A. PREPARING YOUR PRELIMINARY OUTLINE

Following your review of secondary sources, you should have a pretty good understanding of the major issues that are raised by your research problem. At that point it is helpful—after analyzing the issues carefully and considering just how they relate to one another—to prepare a *preliminary outline* that sets out each individual issue and sub-issue you believe you will need to research in order to answer the question presented. (This doesn't necessarily have to be a strict linear outline. If you find it easier to use an alternative method of organizing information, feel free to use that.) As you research each of these issues, you should add citations under each point of the outline to indicate which cases or other authorities support that point. In this way, you "link" your research results to your outline as you proceed with your research.

Suppose, for example, that you have been asked to research the preclusive effect of an earlier court decision on a potential litigation matter under the doctrine of *res judicata* (i.e., claim preclusion). Specifically, your client wants to bring a quiet-title action to establish ownership of a certain piece of land. In an earlier bankruptcy adversary proceeding, the court determined that your client was *not* the owner of the property. Your supervisor now wants you to figure out whether the earlier decision has *res judicata* effect, i.e., whether it precludes your client from bringing the quiet-title action. Your review of secondary sources indicates that there are four requirements in the controlling jurisdiction for *res judicata*: (1) the parties to the two actions must be the same or in privity; (2) the claims in the two actions must be the same; (3) the subject matter of the two actions must be the same; and (4) there must have been a final judgment in the earlier action. Thus, you will need to evaluate whether each of these four requirements is met in order to answer your question presented (i.e., whether the earlier decision precludes the quiet-title action).

Before you begin your search for primary authorities, you should sketch a preliminary outline of the issues, making the four requirements the four sections of your outline. Then, as you find each new authority on point, you should "link" it to one or more of these four major points in your outline. If additional major issues arise in the course of your research, or you find that there are sub-issues that you need to address under a particular point, you should modify your outline accordingly. As the name suggests, your preliminary outline is not a static document. Sometimes the law will turn out to be a little bit different from what you expected, and you will have to modify your outline to conform to unexpected research results.

As you will learn in Chapter 5, your ultimate goal is to have, at the end of your research project, a detailed outline (or similar organizational tool) of all the important issues and sub-issues, linking each point of the outline with the authorities that address that point. Thus, the preliminary outline you prepare in **Step 3** is essentially a prototype for the final outline you produce in **Step 5**, and that outline in turn provides the framework for your final work product.

B. CHOOSING AND PRIORITIZING AMONG PRIMARY SOURCES

After you have prepared a preliminary outline of the major issues, you need to decide which primary sources to research in order to find controlling primary authorities on each issue. Your *research plan* and your review of *secondary sources* should guide you in this determination. Part of developing a research plan, as discussed in Chapter 1, section A, is using your initial understanding of the project and your background knowledge of the law to formulate a strategy for finding legal authorities. Your subsequent review of relevant secondary sources should provide you with additional information about the subject matter and the types of primary authorities that are likely to control the analysis. You should accordingly revise your research plan after reviewing secondary sources if, as is sometimes the case, the law appears to be different from what you initially anticipated.

At that point, you should have a pretty good idea of the types of primary authorities to look for first. If you have a securities-law research problem, for example, and you know from your review of secondary sources that securities-law issues are governed by federal and state statutes and regulations, you would probably want to begin your search for primary authorities with the United States Code or the appropriate state statutory code. If you have a personal injury case involving negligence, on the other hand, you would probably begin your search for primary authorities by looking for cases from the controlling state, since you know that negligence actions are primarily governed by decisional law at the state level. And if you have a zoning issue, your review of secondary sources would likely indicate that local law is controlling, so you would want to begin your search for primary authorities with the relevant municipal code.

Try not to engage in a haphazard review of the various primary sources that ignores the appropriate hierarchy of authority. You want to start your research with the principal type of authority that controls your particular research problem. Though sometimes it is helpful to use an unfiltered electronic word-search just to get a bird's-eye view of all possible types of sources that may be relevant, it is usually best to then use the online filters to narrow your search results to specific sources. Proceeding in this manner makes it easier to analyze the relationships between the various authorities.

On the other hand, don't be overly concerned about making a mistake in selecting the appropriate primary source to look at first. While it's best, for example, to begin a research problem dealing with securities regulation by looking first at the controlling statutory provisions, since that language is paramount, it is not the end of the world if you begin a research problem dealing with securities regulation by looking at some cases, as long as you then go back to look at the relevant statutory scheme once you see that it is cited in the cases. There are more ways than one to go about legal research. And as long as you are diligent, you will probably reach the right result eventually, even if you don't start out in the best place. The various sources of law provide lots of cross-references to other sources, so no matter where you start out, you can end up in the right place.

Still, if you want to be efficient in your research, it helps to start with the main controlling authority and then expand your research from there, rather than having to work backward to the main authority. Progressing systematically like this makes it easier to stay on track and avoid confusion and irrelevant tangents.

C. RESEARCHING PRIMARY AUTHORITIES WITHIN THE PRIMARY SOURCES

After you have prioritized the various sources of primary authority, you are ready to search for relevant primary authorities within those sources. This section discusses how to do that efficiently. (For more information about the individual primary sources themselves, *see* Chapter 9.)

1. STATUTORY RESEARCH

Many research problems revolve around statutory interpretation. If Congress or a state legislature has decided to enact legislation in a particular area of law, then, assuming it is constitutional, the resulting statutory scheme becomes the controlling primary authority within that area of law. While other primary authorities, such as cases and regulations, may have a bearing on how the statute is implemented, interpreted, or applied, they assume a role subordinate to the relevant statute. Thus, if your background knowledge and your review of secondary sources lead you to conclude that the area of law you are researching is or may be controlled by legislation, you will want to start by finding the relevant statutory provision(s).

Secondary sources are a good place to start in determining whether a statute affects an area of law. A good secondary source will tell you whether there is legislation on point in a particular jurisdiction, and if so, it will discuss the effect of the legislation and the interpretations courts have given it. Among secondary sources, loose-leaf services and specialized practice manuals are particularly helpful for researching complex statutory and regulatory issues. (For more on loose-leaf services, *see* Chapter 6, section F, and Chapter 8, section F; for more on specialized practice manuals, *see* Chapter 8, section B.)

You can also search the topical index to a particular jurisdiction's statutory code to see if there are any statutes relevant to the subject matter of your research. And if you are researching online, you can run an electronic word-search in the jurisdiction's statutory database to find statutes by topic. In both cases, you should use the search terms and the electronic word-searches you generated under **Step 1** to conduct your searches (*see* Chapter 1, section B). Remember that if you are researching statutes in print form, you will need to look at the appropriate pocket parts and supplements to find newer cases that interpret the statute, and to see if there have been any recent modifications to the statutory language.

Once you find a statute that addresses your issue, you will need to *expand* your research to see whether there are any other statutes in the code that might affect your analysis as well. You will also want to *update* your research to make sure that the statutory language has not been modified. (For a detailed discussion on expanding and updating statutory research, *see* Chapter 9, section B.)

Next you will want to look at other sources of law to see whether there are any other primary authorities that shed light on the meaning of the statute. Generally you will want to start by determining whether there are any *administrative regulations* implementing the statute. If you use the annotated version of the statute, you will find references to any implementing regulations in the editorial notes at the end of the statutory section, and also in the case annotations. And if you are researching online using WestlawNext or Lexis Advance, the services will automatically generate links to implementing regulations when you pull up the statute. You can also search for any implementing regulations by looking up the statute in the *finding tables* that accompany the index to the applicable regulatory code.

If there are any implementing regulations for the statute, and if they pertain to your research problem, you will next need to expand and update your *regulatory* research, just as you did for your statutory research. (*See* Chapter 9, section D, for a discussion on updating and expanding regulatory research.)

Next, you should search for any *cases* interpreting the relevant statutory language. An easy way to do this is by reviewing the case annotations in the controlling jurisdiction's *annotated code.* These annotations (i.e., case summaries) are arranged by topic for each statutory section, so you can easily see how the courts have interpreted various provisions in the statute. You may also want to use a *citator* (*see* Chapter 8, section H(2)) to see whether there are any additional cases that reference the statute. The disadvantage of using a citator versus an annotated code is that it provides only *citations* to cases rather than case *annotations*, so you have to look at each case to see if it is relevant. But citators cast a wider net, and they also provide the latest information on statutes, so you can see whether there have been any very recent cases or amendments to the statute that have not yet made it into the annotated code.

If you are researching online using one of the principal commercial services, the services automatically generate both annotations and citations for all federal and most state statutes. On WestlawNext, for example, the *Citing References* tab at the top of the page provides all citing cases and other citing references (e.g., secondary sources that cite the statute), and the *Notes of Decisions* tab provides brief annotations of significant cases that interpret the statute.

Normally, once you have found case law in the controlling jurisdiction that addresses your research problem, you will want to move on to **Step 4** (*see* Chapter 4) of the research process to expand and update your case-law research. Note, however, that you can skip Step 4 if your research is confined to statutory interpretation and you have already examined every case listed under the *Citing References* tab, since in that event there will be no other cases that address the statute.

If you have *not* found any controlling cases that answer your question, then you will want to reassess your situation before moving on to **Step 4**. You may want to back up and do some additional background research using *secondary sources* (e.g., a loose-leaf service) to gain a better understanding of the legal framework governing your problem, in order to ensure that you have not missed any relevant cases. If you still come up empty after that, you may want to look for a *persuasive authority* to shed light on the meaning of the relevant statute. (For more on using persuasive authorities, *see* Chapter 7, section G.) Or you might conclude that the plain meaning of the statutory language itself (interpreted in light of any canons of statutory construction the jurisdiction may have adopted) is sufficient to answer your question(s) presented. In any event, you should make sure that you discuss with your supervisor how to proceed in this situation so that you don't spend excessive time on the project.

If your problem is controlled by a *federal statute* and you can't find any controlling cases on point, you would normally want to look for persuasive cases from the other federal courts that interpret the statute. These decisions will be given significant weight by the reviewing court, particularly if their facts are on par with the facts of your research problem.

If your research revolves around a *state statute* and there are no controlling cases (i.e., cases from that state's appellate courts) interpreting it, then you will want to see whether there are any decisions from federal courts in the relevant circuit that interpret the statutory provision. You may also want to look to cases from other jurisdictions that interpret similar statutory provisions for persuasive authority. This is particularly helpful if the controlling state statute tracks a federal statute, in which event you can look to all relevant federal cases for guidance, or if the controlling statute is based on a *model code*, in which you can look to cases from other states that have adopted the language of the model code. But make sure that the language of the statutes in question is sufficiently similar, or cases from other jurisdictions will have little persuasive force.

In addition to persuasive case law, you may want to look at a statute's *legislative history* to shed light on its meaning in the absence of any controlling interpretive cases. This can be complicated, and some (e.g., textualist) judges frown on its use as an interpretive aid. But most judges seem to think that, at least in certain cases, legislative history can be a helpful tool for getting at the legislature's intent in drafting a statute, so you should learn how to make use of it. (*See* Chapter 9, section C for a discussion of when and how to make use of legislative history.)

Another interpretive tool that can sometimes be useful is examining how courts in the controlling jurisdiction have interpreted similar language contained in other statutory provisions in the same code. Suppose, for example, that your client's 15-year-old son was ticketed for driving a golf cart on a street under a certain state statute that prohibits minors below the age of 16 from operating motor vehicles on public streets. Suppose also that there are no cases interpreting the term "motor vehicle" within the meaning of that statute, and that the term is not expressly defined, either in the controlling statute or elsewhere in the code. (If the term *were* defined elsewhere in the code, you could use that definition as persuasive authority for interpreting the same term in the controlling statute. *See* Chapter 7, section G(2).)

In this scenario, you may want to research how courts have interpreted the term "motor vehicle" as it appears in other statutory provisions in the code. Perhaps there is a statute that prohibits operating motor vehicles while intoxicated, and there is a case holding that golf carts are not "motor vehicles" for purposes of that statute. That case would make a helpful persuasive authority that you could use to argue that your client's son did not violate the law concerning the operation of motor vehicles by minors.

There are other persuasive authorities that can be useful for statutory interpretation as well. Attorney General opinions, for example, can be helpful. While not controlling, they give you a good idea of how a statute is likely to be enforced. Also, you may occasionally want to turn to a respected *secondary authority* to help interpret statutory language. (*See* Chapter 2, section D, for more on using secondary sources as persuasive authorities.) Again, however, you should discuss the issue with your supervisor before going too far down the path of persuasive authority.

Once in a while, you may need to research the meaning of a statute not as it reads in its current form, but rather as it existed at an earlier time. Suppose, for example, that your client, a chemical manufacturer, disposed of some toxic waste five years ago, but it was not uncovered until recently. Now the state attorney general wants to pursue your client for fines under a state statute that was amended last year. In order to access your client's liability, you will probably need to research the language of the statute as it was at the time of your client's actions. This will require you to look at an earlier version of the state code, as well as at case law interpreting that earlier language.

You can determine which language in a code was amended at a given time by examining the editorial notes at the end of a given statutory section. In order to find the earlier version of that section (assuming it is not re-printed in the current version), you can check with your reference librarian to see whether your library keeps superseded volumes of codes, either in book form or on microfiche. Or you can look at the historical codes online. The principal online commercial services archive earlier versions of the U.S. Code and individual state codes going back several decades. You can also access free of charge the U.S. Government Publishing Office's *Federal Digital System (FDsys)* website (www.gpo.gov). It retains earlier editions of the U.S. Code back to 1994. Remember that when you look for cases interpreting the earlier statutory language, you will want to focus on cases that have interpreted the language as it was at the relevant time, not as it is in its current form, which means you probably won't be relying on the most recent cases for guidance in interpreting the statutory language.

Finally, there may be times when you want to examine a bill that is pending before Congress or a state legislature, rather than an enacted statute. WestlawNext (*Statutes & Court Rules → Tools & Resources → Bill Tracking*), Bloomberg Law (*Legislation & Regulatory → Search Congressional Bills*), and Lexis Advance (*Browse Sources →* then enter specific search term) all provide ready access to bills pending before Congress. WestlawNext and Lexis Advance also provide access to bills pending before state legislatures, as well as historical collections of bills going back about 20 years. You can search for these bills by entering the bill's number or the title of the bill in the search box, or by using descriptive keywords (e.g., enter "marijuana" to locate bills addressing that topic). There are also several free bill-tracking sources available on the internet. The United States Government Publishing Office's *FDsys* website (www.gpo.gov) carries congressional bills back at least 20 years, as does the Library of Congress's website (www.congress.gov). As for state bills, the Sunlight Foundation's free website (www.sunlight foundation.com → *Tools* → *Other States*) provides a bill-tracking service for relatively recent bills. You can also search for state bills on the websites of the individual state legislatures.

2. REGULATORY RESEARCH

Administrative law (i.e., regulatory law) tends to be quite specialized, particularly at the federal level. Because the various administrative codes are very detailed, practitioners who make administrative law a major part of their practices tend to focus on the rules of particular agencies. Nevertheless, the general researcher will be called upon to find and analyze regulations from time to time. So it is important that you become familiar with regulatory (i.e., administrative) research, even if you do not specialize in administrative law. (For additional background on administrative regulations, *see* Chapter 9, section D.)

If you are looking for regulations as part of a *statutory research problem*, there are several easy ways to determine whether there are any implementing regulations for a given statute. First, you can find the citation(s) for any implementing regulation(s) in the statutory notes that come at the end of every section of an annotated statutory code. Second, in almost all jurisdictions, the index to the applicable *administrative code* will contain finding tables that will enable you to quickly determine whether any regulations have been promulgated pursuant to a particular statute. And if you are researching a statute online, the principal online commercial services will automatically provide references to any implementing regulations.

Sometimes, however, you won't have a citation to an enabling statute to guide your search for implementing regulations. In that event, you can search for the relevant regulations in the applicable administrative code by subject matter, using a *topical index.* The official topical index to the federal administrative code (i.e., the *Code of Federal Regulations,* or "C.F.R.") is called the *C.F.R. Index and Finding Aids,* which is included with the other C.F.R. volumes. There is also an unofficial topical index available, called *West's Code of Federal Regulations General Index*, which is more user-friendly. (An equivalent online index to the C.F.R. is available on WestlawNext, called the *CFR Index.*) As an alternative to using a topical index to find federal regulations, you can run an electronic word-search of the C.F.R. to find any regulations pertaining to your topic. This search capability is available on the principal online commercial services, as well as on the Government Publishing Office's free *FDsys* website (www.gpo.gov).

Once you have found regulations relevant to your research problem, you should carefully read the language of the *enabling statute* (i.e., the statute that gives the agency authority to promulgate the regulations) so that you understand the purpose of the regulations and the context in which they were enacted. You can generally find a citation to the enabling statute in the Editorial Notes at the end of the regulatory provision in question. Remember also that the scope of an agency's rule-making cannot legally exceed its delegated authority under the enabling statute; if it does, your client may have grounds for challenging the validity of the implementing regulations.

Next you will need to *expand* your research to see if there are any other regulations in the code that might also have a bearing on your analysis. And then you will need to *update* your research to make sure that the regulations you found are still valid and have not been modified. (*See* Chapter 9, section D, for a discussion on how to expand and update your regulatory research.)

After expanding and updating your regulatory research, you should then look to see whether there are any *court cases* or *administrative decisions* interpreting the regulations. Decisional law is important in construing regulations, just as it is in construing statutes. A specialized loose-leaf service is a good place to start; it will provide annotations of important interpretive decisions. (*See* Chapter 8, section F, for a discussion of loose-leaf services.) You can also use a *citator* (*see* Chapter 8, section H(2)) to view all the cases that have cited the regulation. Keep in mind, though, that a citator provides only citations, not annotations.

If you are looking at a regulation using one of the principal online commercial services, the service will automatically generate a list of citing cases and administrative decisions. On WestlawNext, for example, the *Citing References* tab at the top of the page provides all citing cases and administrative decisions, along with other citing references (e.g., secondary sources that cite the regulation). And the *Notes of Decisions* tab provides brief annotations of significant interpretive court cases.

If you do find interpretive cases or administrative decisions that address your research problem, you will normally want to move on to **Step 4** of the research process (*see* Chapter 4) to expand and update your case research. Note, however, that you can skip Step 4 if your research is confined to regulatory interpretation and you have already examined every decision listed under the *Citing References* tab, since in that event there will be no other decisions that address the regulation.

If you do not find any cases or decisions that address your research problem, or if the regulations are central to your analysis, you may want to pursue more in-depth regulatory research by looking for other agency-specific sources (e.g. agency manuals, policy statements, and advisory letters) that can provide further guidance as to the meaning and applicability of the regulations. These types of documents can shed light on the agency's own interpretation of its regulations, and you can sometimes use that information to argue that the agency is estopped from taking a different interpretation with respect to your client's case.

Finally, there may be times, as in the case of statutory research, where your client's situation is governed by an earlier version of a regulation, rather than the current version, because the relevant events took place prior to the enactment of the current version. In that event, you will need to look at an earlier version of the administrative code, as well as at case law interpreting that earlier language.

You can determine which language in a regulatory code was amended and at what time by examining the editorial notes at the end of a given regulatory provision. In order to find an earlier version of the C.F.R., you can use the Government Publishing Office's free *FDsys* website (www.gpo.gov), which retains earlier editions of the C.F.R. back to 1996, or you can use WestlawNext or Lexis Advance, which both archive earlier editions of the C.F.R. back several decades. Finding an earlier version of a particular *state's* administrative code may be trickier. You can check with your reference librarian to see whether your law library keeps superseded volumes of state administrative codes, either in book form or on microfiche. Or use WestlawNext and Lexis Advance, which have limited collections of archived state administrative codes going back at least 10 years. You can also look at the applicable agency's website, or try contacting the state agency directly.

Remember that when you are looking for cases interpreting older regulations, you will want to focus on cases that interpreted the language as it was at the relevant time, not as it is in its current form, which means you probably won't be relying on the most recent cases. (For more information on regulatory research, *see* Chapter 9, section D.)

3. CASE-LAW RESEARCH

As discussed in the preceding two sections, researching cases is an important part of statutory and regulatory research. In addition, for some types of research projects, you will want to *start* your search for primary authorities with case law, rather than, say, a statute or regulation. Normally this will be in situations where your review of secondary sources in **Step 2** (*see* Chapter 2, section A) leads you to the conclusion that the area of law you are researching (e.g., the tort of intentional infliction of emotional distress) is controlled principally by case law rather than a statute, regulation, or other textual authority.

Often, the secondary sources themselves will point you directly to controlling case law. Practice manuals are particularly helpful for this, as are A.L.R.'s and specialized loose-leaf services. (*See* Chapter 8 for more on these secondary sources.) In addition to secondary sources, there are two principal tools lawyers have traditionally used to find cases by subject matter: (1) digests and (2) electronic word-searches. Even if you have found some relevant cases through your review of secondary sources, you will normally want to use one or both of these other tools to locate additional cases on point before proceeding to **Step 4**. As always, it is better to err on the side of redundancy, if time and resources allow.

Digests were the traditional tool for finding cases by subject matter prior to the advent of electronic research services. Prepared by West Publishing, they compile short abstracts of court decisions ("annotations") and organize them alphabetically by topic. If an annotation looks promising, you can then review the case in its full form in the appropriate case reporter.

Different digests compile case annotations for different jurisdictions. Use the search terms you generated in **Step 1** (*see* Chapter 1, section B(1)) to access the digest's topical index (called the *Descriptive Word Index*), which will direct you to case annotations on your subject matter. Or if you already have a case on point, you can use the *key number* in the headnote to locate other cases on that same point of law. West Publishing assigns a unique key number to many thousands of different points of law. This tool is very helpful for finding cases on the same issue across jurisdictions. Thus, if you found a case on point in a treatise, but it is not from the controlling jurisdiction, you can use the *West Key Number System* to see whether there are any cases on point in the controlling jurisdiction. (For more on using key numbers to find cases across jurisdictions, *see* Chapter 4, section B, and Chapter 8, section H(1).)

The principal online commercial services do not carry digests *per se*, but they do have digest functionality that allows you to search for cases by topic (i.e., subject matter). On WestlawNext, you can search by topic by clicking on the *Key Numbers* tab in the main directory. On Lexis Advance, you can search by topic by clicking on the *Browse* tab at the top of the page, and then the *Topic* tab underneath it. You can then choose from an alphabetical index of topics and subtopics to find your issue. After you select a topic, you can select one or more jurisdictions to search within, and you also have the option of adding additional search terms to customize your search within the designated topic. (For more on using the online digest functions for WestlawNext and Lexis Advance, *see* Chapter 8, section H(1).)

These days, however, the principal tool lawyers use to find cases is the *electronic word-search*. Electronic word-searches are fast and powerful, but there are some downsides to their use as well. First, they can be more expensive, though the cost varies significantly among the various providers and is generally going down over time. (For more on research costs, as well as an overview of the various online commercial services available, *see* Chapter 6, section C.) Second, electronic word-searches can be a little tricky, particularly for the novice, because it is fairly easy for the researcher to get off track. When you find cases by topic using a *digest*, or its online equivalent, you know that you are generally in the ballpark because your search has progressed logically from a more general topic to a more specific topic, and you get a feel for that area of law and how your problem relates to it. With electronic word-searches, on the other hand, your research lacks that background and context, so it is easier to go astray and get off on a tangent. Nevertheless, electronic word-searching can be more efficient than digest searching, if you craft your searches skillfully.

Careful crafting of search terms is particularly important if you are using *terms-and-connectors* word-searches (*see* Chapter 1, section B(2)). These enable very precise searches, and they are very effective if you use them properly. But their downside is that they are rather unforgiving. If you make even a minor error in formulating your search terms, it can render your search ineffective. So you have to craft terms-and-connectors searches carefully and be willing to modify them if they turn out to be overly broad (i.e., pulling up too many cases), or alternatively, overly narrow (resulting in few or no relevant cases). The online commercial services have tools to help you construct terms-and-connectors searches, if you are not confident about how to do so. (For suggestions on how to narrow and expand electronic word-searches, *see* Chapter 1, section B(2), and Chapter 7, sections D and E.)

You should focus on answering your *question presented* when you look for case law, rather than on finding every possible case that relates in any way to the issue. (*See* Chapter 6, section H, for more on focusing your research efforts on results.) Once you have found some relevant controlling authorities, be sure to analyze the facts and the holdings carefully to ensure that the cases are really responsive to your question presented. If they are, then you can proceed to **Step 4** (*see* Chapter 4) to *expand* and *update* your case-law research.

Before you move on to **Step 4** of your research, however, you should also check whether there are any *statutes* that bear on your case-law issue. (*See* section C(1) of this chapter for more on statutory research.) Normally, you would expect to see any relevant legislation referenced in the cases or the secondary sources you reviewed, but if you are not sure, it is best to a take quick look at the topical index to the annotated code and to run an electronic search of the code to make sure that you haven't missed anything. Increasingly, legislation affects areas of law that have traditionally been left to the courts, such as tort law, and you'll definitely need to know whether Congress or a state legislature has weighed in on the area of law you are researching.

If your search for controlling cases on point comes up empty, you'll first want to consider whether your searches were flawed (*see* Chapter 1, section B). You may also want to go back to one or more secondary sources to make sure you understand the basic legal landscape adequately (*see* Chapter 2, section E). And if you relied exclusively on either electronic word-searches or subject-matter searches to find relevant cases, you may want to search again with the other tool. This is particularly important if you have relied on terms-and-connectors searches exclusively, since your lack of search results may be due to poorly crafted searches, rather than to a lack of case law. (For more on what to do if you cannot find relevant authorities, *see* Chapter 7, section D.)

If you've searched for controlling cases using both subject-matter searches and electronic word-searches, and you still can't find a case on point, you should consider searching for *persuasive cases* from other jurisdictions. A case from another jurisdiction that is on point and factually similar to your case can be quite persuasive in the absence of any controlling cases. You may also want to use a *secondary source* for persuasive authority if there are no persuasive *cases* on point. (For more on using persuasive authorities generally, *see* Chapter 7, section G; for more on using secondary sources as persuasive authorities, *see* Chapter 2, section D.)

4. RESEARCHING OTHER TYPES OF PRIMARY AUTHORITIES

If your review of secondary sources **(Step 2)** leads you to begin your search for primary authorities with a textual authority other than a statute or a regulation, you should follow the same basic procedures as you would for researching those types of authorities. First, you will need to find and analyze the language of the controlling text. (For further information on finding various types of primary authorities, *see* Chapter 9.) Then you will need to *expand* and *update* your research. And lastly, you will want to look for *decisional law* that interprets the textual language.

Expanding your research for most other types of primary authorities, such as municipal codes and court rules, is similar to expanding your research for statutes and regulations. Basically it just involves reviewing the neighboring provisions in the applicable document for relevance, and then searching the rest of the code or compilation (using a topical index, a table of contents, and probably also an electronic word-search) to see whether there are any other provisions on point.

Updating your research for these types of textual authorities means (1) seeing whether the language of the provision has changed, and (2) making sure the authority is still valid. As in the case of statutes and regulations, this process is usually automatic if you are using one of the principal online commercial services, as these services continually update the sources they carry. On the other hand, if you are researching a source in print, or using a free online source, you will need to verify that the source you are working with is still current.

Next, you will want to search for any *cases* (starting with controlling cases) that would shed light on the meaning of the controlling language. If you find court cases that interpret the primary authority, you can move on to **Step 4** to expand and update your case research (*see* Chapter 4). If you *cannot* find any cases on point, then you will need to decide (and discuss with your supervisor) whether you can rely on the language of the controlling primary authority itself to resolve your research problem, or whether you should continue to search for other interpretive authorities.

Suppose, for example, that your research problem involves a federal constitutional issue. You will want to start your search for primary authorities by reviewing and analyzing the applicable provision in the United States Constitution. (I'm assuming here that you have already followed **Steps 1 and 2**; secondary sources are particularly important when it comes to constitutional research.) You should then search for cases interpreting the applicable provision, perhaps by reviewing annotations in the United States Code Annotated. You would look first for any U.S. Supreme Court cases, and then for appeals-court cases in the controlling circuit. If you find one or more controlling cases on point, you can move on to **Step 4**. If you don't, you will probably want to look for persuasive cases in other circuits and from the federal district courts. If you don't find any persuasive cases on point, then you would want to consider (and discuss with your supervisor) whether to research *historical materials* (e.g., records of the proceedings at the Constitutional Convention and records of the state-ratification debates) that might shed light on the meaning of the constitutional language. (For more on using persuasive authorities generally, *see* Chapter 7, section G; for more on constitutions and constitutional research, *see* Chapter 9, section A.)

Suppose, on the other hand, that instead of a lofty constitutional issue, your research problem involves a rather mundane local matter, such as an animal-licensing requirement. (Perhaps your client was ticketed for not displaying a valid dog tag on her schnauzer while walking the dog through a city park.) Most likely, after a quick review of a state-specific legal encyclopedia or other secondary source, you would decide that the matter is governed by the city's municipal code. You would then start your search for primary authorities by locating (probably on the city's website) the municipal code and analyzing the applicable provisions. After that, you would need to *expand* your research by looking for other code provisions on point, and you would need to *update* your research by making sure that the version of the municipal code you are looking at is current.

Then you would likely want to look for decisional law interpreting the relevant ordinance. It is possible that through an online search you could find a reported court case discussing the ordinance, though that is not likely. The more likely scenario is that any decision shedding light on the relevant ordinance is going to come from a local court or agency, and that it will be unpublished. (Some municipalities, such as New York City, do publish such decisions, but most do not.) So you would likely have to dig around a bit to find any local decisions. You could, for example, start with the website of the relevant municipality or agency to find the names of the appropriate records clerk; then contact that person for information on how to access unpublished local decisions.

If you do find one or more unpublished local decisions on point, you probably won't be able to update them under **Step 4** because they generally are not covered by the citators. You also cannot cite them as precedents, because they do not have binding effect. Local decisions can nevertheless be helpful in seeing how an ordinance or regulation has been interpreted in the past, which can help you predict how it would likely be applied in the future.

If you cannot locate any relevant local decisions, then you would need to assess (and discuss with your supervisor) whether it is worth digging even further for other types of interpretive documents, such as local departmental manuals or policy statements.

To research other types of primary authorities (e.g., court rules), you will want to proceed in a like manner. It is important to first analyze the language of the controlling authority. Next you will want to expand and update your research, as described above. And then you will want to look for cases that interpret the relevant language. If you find cases on point, then you can move on to **Step 4**, expanding and (if possible) updating your case research. And if you cannot locate any decisions on point, then you will need to decide (in conjunction with your supervisor) whether the importance of the project justifies digging further for other types of interpretive documents that may shed light on the meaning of the relevant language, or whether you can comfortably rely on the controlling language itself to resolve your research problem.

CHAPTER 4

STEP 4: EXPAND AND UPDATE YOUR CASE RESEARCH

■ ■ ■

A. Examining Your Cases for References to Earlier Relevant Cases

B. Using Key Numbers to Find Additional Relevant Cases

C. Using a Citator to Update and Validate Your Case Research

D. Expanding and Updating Your Research for Other Types of Primary Authorities

A common mistake newer researchers often make is failing to fully *expand* and *update* their case research. Yet this step is important to making sure that your research results are complete and current. So before you move on to **Step 5** to analyze and organize your research, you should take the necessary measures to ensure that you have found all the significant cases that are on point. This chapter discusses those measures.

A. EXAMINING YOUR CASES FOR REFERENCES TO EARLIER RELEVANT CASES

You should start the process by examining the cases you have already found for references to earlier cases on point. Often, you will discover that the cases you found in your initial search rely on, or at least cite, some other relevant cases that you did not uncover. If these cited cases appear from the context of your citing case to be on point, then you should review them to see whether in fact they address your issue. If so, then you should consider incorporating them into your research results.

Whether you actually include such cases in your research results will depend in large part on the types of cases they are and how they relate to what you have already found. For example, if you have found a controlling state-supreme-court case on point, and it cites a decision from another state, the latter case probably won't be of much help to you, unless for some reason you need a persuasive authority (*see* Chapter 7, section G, for more on persuasive authorities). Similarly, if it cites an *older* supreme-court case from the controlling state, that won't generally add anything, unless the older case is seminal, or is closer to your problem on the facts.

On the other hand, if you have found several court-of-appeals cases from the controlling jurisdiction in your initial research, and one of them cites a supreme-court case you haven't looked at, you will definitely want to check the supreme-court case to see whether it is germane to your research problem. Or, supposing you have found three court-of-appeals cases roughly on point, but none is very close to your problem on the facts, you may want to check their citations to earlier cases to see if any of these earlier cases is closer on the facts. If so, then you would probably want to include the case(s) that is closer on the facts with your research results. (*See* Chapter 5, section A(2) for a further discussion of prioritizing your final research results.)

B. USING KEY NUMBERS TO FIND ADDITIONAL RELEVANT CASES

Another helpful way to expand your case research is to take advantage of West's *Key Number System.* This is an important feature of West's American Digest System that links that system to West's National Reporter System. As discussed further in Chapter 8, section H(1), the Key Number System divides the law into approximately 400 major legal topics for purposes of its digest system and arranges them alphabetically. It then divides and subdivides these topics into smaller and smaller categories that ultimately reduce to individual points of law (approximately 100,000 in all), each identified by its own unique "key number" (or more accurately, by its own unique topic and key number).

If you look at a case from a West Publishing reporter, you'll see that the editors have added *headnotes* that summarize the various legal topics discussed in the case, and next to each headnote you will see one or more key-shaped symbols with a topic and number next to it. Those are the key numbers. The most specific key number corresponds to the particular point of law discussed in the headnote. Thus, if you have found a case that is responsive to your research problem, you can use its unique key number to find other cases on that point of law, either in the same jurisdiction or in any other jurisdiction.

Suppose, for example, that you are researching Florida law regarding the privilege defense to the tort of intentional infliction of emotional distress ("IIED"), and you have found a case in your preliminary research that is right on point: *Metropolitan Life Ins. Co. v. McCarson*, 467 So. 2d 277 (Fla. 1985). By looking at the headnotes to that case, you see that headnote No. 2 summarizes the court's holding that the defendant insurer is not liable to the plaintiff for IIED because its actions were privileged. Above this headnote, you will see (on WestlawNext) two links next to "key" symbols, one of which is *Privilege or Immunity; Exercise of Legal Rights.* Clicking on that link takes you to summaries (i.e. annotations) of cases that discuss that topic, which is assigned the key number *Damages 115K57.49.* The beauty of West's Key Number System is that you can use this key number (*Damages 115K57.49*) to find other cases on the same point, anywhere in the United States, by just selecting the appropriate jurisdiction from the drop-down menu. (Likewise, if you are researching in print, that key number will enable you to find cases on the same topic in whichever digest you select.)

One important point to remember when using key numbers to expand your research is that the editors do not always catalogue cases exactly as you might think they would. So it is helpful to search for cases using several related key numbers (WestlawNext lets you combine them easily by clicking the appropriate boxes), rather than just the one that looks to be on point, to ensure that you don't miss any relevant cases.

If you are expanding your Florida research on the privilege defense to IIED, for example, you might want to search under *Damages 115K57.19*, which is the general key number corresponding to the broader topic of IIED, as well as *Damages 115K57.49*, which is the more specific key number corresponding to the topic of privilege. Or you might try looking under one or more related key numbers, such as *Damages 115K57.21*, which corresponds to the topic "Elements of IIED, generally," to capture more cases.

If you are researching in print, you can locate the key numbers for a particular topic by looking up your specific topic in the Descriptive Word Index. If you are researching on WestlawNext, start by clicking on the *Key Numbers* tab in the main directory. You can then locate the key numbers for your specific topic either by using search terms or by drilling down through the outline. Remember, for purposes of expanding your research, it is better to err on the side of finding too many cases than too few, so don't hesitate to try multiple key numbers.

Getting accustomed to using the West Key Number System can take a little practice. But once you get used to it, the system is easy to use, particularly the online version. And it is a helpful tool for expanding your case research, especially if you have relied exclusively on electronic word-searches for your preliminary research in **Step 3**.

C. USING A CITATOR TO UPDATE AND VALIDATE YOUR CASE RESEARCH

After you have expanded your research by reviewing your existing cases for references to earlier cases, and perhaps also by using the West Key Number System to look at digest annotations on the topic, you should then use a *case citator* to find more recent authorities on point, and to make sure that your existing cases (and other primary authorities) are still valid. (There are three principal citators: WestlawNext has *KeyCite*, Lexis Advance has *Shepard's,* and Bloomberg Law has *BCite*.) This is probably the most important part of **Step 4**.

Many beginning researchers mistakenly assume that citators are useful only to verify that their cases and other authorities are still valid (*see* Chapter 6, section J). But they are also valuable research tools, as they provide citing references to all of the cases and other authorities (including secondary sources) that mention your authorities. Thus, they are helpful for finding other, more recent authorities on the same topic.

When you update a case using a citator, the *headnotes* of the case are particularly important. Each headnote in a case identifies a specific point of law, and the headnotes are numbered consecutively. When you check a case using a citator, the citator will tell you what later cases have cited the case you entered. Moreover, the citator will usually indicate what specific points of law from your original case those citing cases discuss. Thus, if you found the *McCarson* case discussed above in section B of this chapter as part of your research, and if Headnote 2 of that case discusses the point of law that is relevant to your research problem, then you can use a citator to find other, later cases that cite *McCarson* and are relevant to the same point of law that *McCarson* discusses in Headnote 2.

To do this, click on the *Citing References* link if you are using KeyCite, the *Citing Decisions* link if you are using Shepard's, or the *Citing Decisions* link if you are using BCite. Then look for a symbol for Headnote #2 next to the citations listed. (Or, you can reach the same result by just clicking on the link next to the relevant headnote in the case that says there are "x cases that cite this headnote".) This tells you that the citing case not only cites *McCarson,* but that it also discusses the same point of law that was discussed in headnote [2] of *McCarson.*

By using a citator in this manner, you can find all the later cases, from every jurisdiction (or you can look at a particular jurisdiction), that have cited your original cases (i.e., those you found in **Step 3**) and have discussed the same points of law. If after reviewing these cases you determine that some of them are indeed responsive to your research problem, then you should check the citing references for them as well to see if there are any still-later cases from the controlling jurisdiction that discuss the same point of law. And you should keep doing this with each new case you find that is on point until there are no more recent cases to check. At that point, you will have thoroughly updated your case research.

Note that some of the citing cases listed don't have any headnote-numbers next to them, so you won't be able to tell without reading these cases what points of law they discuss. But if a case is important to your analysis, you should probably take a look at all of the citing cases from the controlling jurisdiction, just to make sure you don't miss any significant cases. (For more on using a citator to update your research, *see* Chapter 8, section H(2).)

Finally, as noted above, in addition to using a citator to *update* your case research, you also need to use the citator to make sure that all cases and other primary authorities you plan to rely on are still *valid* and have not, for example, been overruled or reversed. (*See* Chapter 8, section H(2), if you are not sure how to do this.) And if it's been a little while since you validated a case, or you are not sure whether you've validated it already, check it again. It never hurts to validate all your cases again at the end of your research, as there are few worse fates for the legal researcher than turning in a work product that relies on an invalid authority. (For more on the importance of validating your authorities, *see* Chapter 6, section J.)

D. EXPANDING AND UPDATING YOUR RESEARCH FOR OTHER TYPES OF PRIMARY AUTHORITIES

In addition to expanding and updating your *case* research, it is also necessary to expand and update your research for statutes, regulations, and other types of primary authorities to ensure (1) that you have found all related provisions on point, and (2) that the relevant language of the text you are relying on is current. However, there is generally less involved in expanding and updating these types of textual authorities. And since the updating process is largely automatic if you are using one of the principal online commercial services, this book covers the expanding and updating process for statutes, regulations, and other types of primary authorities in Chapter 3, which discusses the research process generally for these sources. Thus, if you have properly followed the procedures set out in Chapter 3, your initial research on statutes, regulations, and other textual authorities should already be complete and up-to-date. (For a more detailed discussion on expanding and updating your statutory and regulatory research, *see* Chapter 9, sections B and D; for a discussion on expanding and updating your research for other types of textual authorities, *see* Chapter 3, section C(4).)

Remember that in addition to expanding and updating your research for statutes, regulations, and other textual authorities, such as court rules and municipal ordinances, you will also want to look for decisional law (and perhaps other authorities) to interpret the meaning of the controlling language. (*See* Chapter 3, sections C(1), C(2), and C(4), for more on this topic.)

CHAPTER 5

STEP 5: ANALYZE AND ORGANIZE YOUR RESEARCH RESULTS

■ ■ ■

A. Analyzing Your Research Results
   1. Pruning Tangential Authorities
   2. Prioritizing and Harmonizing Cases
      (a) Prioritizing Cases
      (b) Harmonizing Cases
   3. Evaluating Your Answer
B. Organizing Your Research Results

Your last step in any research project involves thinking carefully about your research results. There are two aspects to this. First, you need to carefully *analyze* your research results. Hopefully, you have done some of this in **Step 3 and Step 4**, as you decided which authorities were relevant to your research problem. But it is important before you move on to preparing your ultimate work product that you undertake a further, more detailed analysis of your research to make sure that you have garnered the best possible support for your conclusion(s), and that you have carefully evaluated how these authorities address your research problem. Second, you need to *organize* your research results, integrating them into your *final outline*. Taking the time to assess your research results in this manner will greatly facilitate a smooth transition from your research project to your ultimate work product.

A. ANALYZING YOUR RESEARCH RESULTS

There are three discreet tasks involved in analyzing your research results. First, you should endeavor to prune away those that are not really on point; second, you should give some thought to prioritizing and harmonizing those that remain; and finally, you should evaluate carefully whether your analysis of your final research results provides an appropriate answer to your question(s) presented. Each of these tasks is discussed in turn below.

1. PRUNING TANGENTIAL AUTHORITIES

First, it is important to scrutinize the authorities you've found to make sure that they are really on point. Sometimes your research will lead you down pathways that end up being tangential to your question presented. And sometimes the direction of your research changes a bit as you learn more about an area of law. Furthermore, with *case law* there are often subtleties in the facts or the holdings that upon closer reading render them inapposite to your analysis. So you need to read each authority you plan to rely on carefully to make sure that it is really germane to your analysis and not just tangentially related.

At times in my legal-writing class, for example, I use a civil assault problem for one of my memo assignments. Invariably, there are students who rely heavily and unreflectively on criminal cases in their analyses of civil assault, even though the legal standards for criminal assault and civil assault are a bit different. While criminal cases may have *some* bearing on a civil analysis, they need to be employed cautiously, and the issue should be brought to the reader's attention. Using such cases unreflectively indicates that the student has not subjected his or her research to careful analysis to ensure that it is truly responsive to the questions the memo is supposed to address.

So think carefully about whether there is anything about your authorities that would make them inapplicable, and in particular about whether the facts of a given case are just too different from your research scenario to make the case useful for your purposes, even if the general subject matter is relevant.

2. PRIORITIZING AND HARMONIZING CASES

The next task is to *prioritize* and *harmonize* the case law you found in your research. By prioritizing cases, I mean that if you have multiple cases that stand for the same rule, you should decide which of them you want to rely on in your analysis. By harmonizing cases, I mean that you need to analyze seemingly conflicting holdings and determine how they relate to each other.

(a) Prioritizing Cases

While it is sometimes helpful to cite multiple cases on an important point, it is usually best not to overwhelm the reader with a lot of lengthy string citations, as this needlessly disrupts the flow of your writing. Thus, you should cite no more cases than you need to make your point effectively. So if you have found multiple cases on the same point, you will need to decide which one(s) to use in your analysis.

Suppose, for example, that you have a fairly recent state-supreme-court decision on a certain point of law, and that it affirms several earlier appeals-court decisions. There is generally no advantage to including all the citations in a string cite to support that point. The supreme-court decision alone is sufficient. (An exception would be where one of the lower-court cases is more on par factually with your case; in that scenario you would probably want to cite both the supreme-court decision and the most applicable appeals-court decision.) In choosing which case(s) to rely on in situations where you have found multiple cases on the same point, you should look to several factors, including the factual similarity with your research problem, which court decided the case (*see also* the discussion below regarding case hierarchy), and, to a lesser extent, the age of the case, and the depth and significance of the court's analysis. (*See* Chapter 7, section K, for more on choosing the "best" cases to support your analysis.)

The first factor, factual similarity, is one beginning researchers tend to under-emphasize. They tend to want to apply legal rules to the facts abstractly, without adequately comparing or contrasting the facts of the precedent to the facts of their own problem. But legal analysis is as much about stories as rules. Thus, if you can show a court that your case is factually on par with a particular precedent, it is much more persuasive than just trying to apply the rule of the precedent abstractly to your own factual scenario. So factual analysis is vital when you are prioritizing your research results.

(b) Harmonizing Cases

The need to *harmonize* decisions arises when you have multiple cases addressing a point of law, but they stand for rules that are different, or even contrasting. In that situation you will want to evaluate how the holdings relate to each other, which will determine how you should use them. One case, for example, may state a general rule, while two others on the same topic explicitly carve out exceptions to the general rule. You will need to be clear on these relationships before you prepare your final outline of your research results (which is discussed below in section B of this chapter).

Harmonizing case law is particularly important when you have cases that are factually similar but appear to present conflicting holdings on a point of law. In that situation, you will generally want to try to harmonize the holdings by synthesizing a rule that gives a consistent reading to the seemingly disparate cases. Normally, this will mean that one case stands for a general rule, and the other case carves out an exception to the rule that applies in certain factual circumstances.

But occasionally you may instead decide (particularly if you are writing a persuasive brief) that one case is consistent with the controlling law, and the other simply is not. It could be, for example, that the earlier holding is now outdated and is no longer a controlling authority; or it could be that one holding is from another jurisdiction, and that jurisdiction follows a different legal rule. The ability to make these determinations and deal deftly with conflicting holdings is part of what sets the first-rate researcher apart from the ordinary researcher. It requires you to be skilled in *case synthesis*, and it requires you to understand the complexities of *case hierarchy*.

Case synthesis is an intellectual endeavor whereby a lawyer attempts to reconcile and rationalize disparate holdings so that they stand for a consistent legal principle. It requires the researcher to analyze which facts are legally significant, and then create a new rule "synthetically" to encompass the holdings and factual backgrounds of the decisions. As noted above, when the holdings reach different results, case synthesis usually entails limiting one of the holdings to its specific factual context, so that it stands for an exception to a more general rule encompassed by the other holding.

Suppose, for example, that you have two precedents from the same court involving liability on the part of golfers for inadvertently hitting other golfers with errant shots. The older case, without discussing the negligence doctrine in depth, holds that the offending golfer is *not* liable for the resulting injury because golfers assume the risk of being hit by errant golf balls as a condition of playing the game. The more recent case, without distinguishing the first case or analyzing the assumption-of-risk doctrine it relies on, holds that the offending golfer *is* liable because he was negligent in not calling out "fore" when the ball approached the hapless victim, who had his back turned to the offending golfer.

To reconcile these seemingly conflicting holdings, you would need to synthesize a rule, not fully expressed in either case, that encompasses both holdings. One possibility would be to formulate a rule that golfers can be liable for hitting other golfers with errant shots, but only in circumstances where the victim golfer has his back turned (and accordingly cannot see the ball coming), and where the offending golfer fails to yell "fore" or otherwise warn the victim golfer while the ball is in the air.

There is not necessarily one "right" way to synthesize cases; reasonable lawyers can and do disagree in these situations as to how broadly the existing precedents should be read and what the controlling rule should be. As a result, case synthesis requires some creativity on the part of the lawyer, and a sense for how a court would likely apply the holdings to a new factual scenario. The indefiniteness of this enterprise contributes significantly to the intellectual challenge and creativity of practicing law.

The other principal factor that bears on harmonizing disparate case law is *case hierarchy*. Considerations of case hierarchy arise where seemingly conflicting cases have different precedential value—where, for example, one case is from the supreme court of the controlling jurisdiction, and the other is a case from another jurisdiction, or from a federal court interpreting state law. In these situations, synthesizing the cases is more subtle, and in some circumstances the legal researcher needs to give consideration to simply disregarding the non-controlling case because it does not state the law of the controlling jurisdiction.

Suppose, for example, that in the hypothetical case discussed above, the precedents are from different states. The case finding *no liability* on the part of the offending golfer is a state-supreme-court case from Arkansas, which is the controlling jurisdiction. And the case *finding liability* is from the Georgia Supreme Court. What then? Basically you have two choices. On the one hand you could simply conclude that the law of the two states is different, and that in Arkansas there is no liability for injuries caused by errant golf shots. Or alternatively, you could try to harmonize the cases by reasoning that the Arkansas Supreme Court would likely have reached the same result that the Georgia Supreme Court did (and thus have found liability) *if* it had been confronted with a similar factual scenario. In that way, you would try to synthesize the two cases to come up with a narrow exception to the general no-liability rule in Arkansas.

In a litigation matter, your choice between these options would depend upon which side of the dispute you were on. If you represented the victim golfer (i.e., the one hit by the ball), you would try to synthesize the rules by arguing for a negligence exception to the general no-liability rule. You would then try to distinguish the controlling Arkansas decision on its facts and argue that the negligence exception carved out by the Georgia decision properly applies in this particular factual context. Conversely, if you represented the offending golfer (i.e., the one who hit the errant shot), you would argue in favor of disregarding the Georgia case, notwithstanding its factual parity with the instant case, on the grounds that Arkansas simply followed a different legal rule from that followed in Georgia. Again, there is no obviously correct interpretation in this situation; the reviewing court could reasonably go either way, and that gives both sides room to formulate plausible arguments.

The situation is complicated further if the disparate decisions arise from different courts in the same jurisdiction. Suppose the case finding liability for the errant golf shot is from a federal district court in Arkansas, and the case finding no liability is from the Arkansas Supreme Court. In that type of scenario, a reviewing court would have a stronger incentive to try to reconcile the two cases instead of simply disregarding the non-controlling federal case that carves out an exception for negligence, because courts within the same state have an interest in trying to harmonize their decisions. Even so, since the federal case finding negligence is merely persuasive authority, it remains open to the reviewing court weighing the two decisions cases to construe the federal case narrowly on its facts, so that it stands for only a very limited exception to the general no-liability rule—an exception that would not apply in the instant case.

A somewhat similar type of scenario is presented where two seemingly conflicting precedents, neither of which has been expressly overruled, come from the same court, but one is significantly *older* than the other. Again, a reviewing court will generally try to harmonize the cases out of respect for precedent, but it may instead confine the earlier case narrowly to its facts. And occasionally courts have held that the reasoning of earlier precedents should no longer be followed, even if they were never expressly overruled.

These kinds of considerations are subtle and difficult, and sometimes there are no easy answers as to how you should deal with conflicting cases. But it is important to try to work through these issues in your final analysis, so as to eliminate any waffling and confusion in your ultimate conclusion, and to anticipate any possible counterarguments.

3. EVALUATING YOUR ANSWER

The final analytical step, after you have pruned tangential cases and then prioritized and harmonized your remaining authorities, is to evaluate whether you have adequately answered your question presented. Probably the best way to do this is to prepare a *short answer* to it. If you find that your research results allow you to summarize in a paragraph or two a succinct and accurate answer to the question presented, then you can be reasonably confident that you have solved your research problem. If you find that you cannot succinctly and accurately answer the question presented, then that is a good indication that your research is not yet complete. Preparing a short answer is also helpful because it helps you to distill your research results down to their essential points.

If after a careful analysis of your authorities you find that you cannot prepare an adequate short answer, then you will probably need to do some additional research.

For starters, you may need to go back and revisit your search terms or your electronic word-searches (*see* Chapter 1, section B) to make them more responsive to your question presented. (For guidance on how to proceed if you do this and still can't find any controlling authorities, *see* Chapter 7, section D.)

Unless you are working under a particular time or budgetary constraint, you will normally want to keep digging, either until you find a controlling authority that answers your question presented, or until (and this doesn't happen all that often) you satisfy yourself after a thorough effort that there simply are not any controlling authorities out there that provide an answer to your question presented. In that case, you may want to look to the law of other jurisdictions or to secondary sources as persuasive authority. (*See* Chapter 7, section G, for more on persuasive authority.) You should consult with your supervisor, however, before undertaking extensive research for persuasive authorities, to ensure that your research is properly focused and to ensure that the project justifies the additional expenditure of time. (For more on the need to maintain communication with your supervisor as you proceed with your research, *see* Chapter 6, section B.)

In the event you cannot find even a persuasive authority on point, you should sit down with your supervisor and discuss how to proceed. Depending on the assignment and the client's needs, your supervisor may be satisfied with an inconclusive answer. Or your supervisor may suggest other angles for you to consider in looking for authorities, or she may want you to use tangentially related cases creatively to make an argument by analogy. The latter possibility is likely to occur in an adversarial context, where, for example, your supervisor is preparing a brief and needs to come up with *some* kind of reasonable argument in support of the client's position, even if there are no obvious authorities on point. (*See* Chapter 6, section I, for more on the importance of persistence in legal research.)

B. ORGANIZING YOUR RESEARCH RESULTS

The second important component of **Step 5** is *organizing* your research results. This should be relatively easy if you have followed the steps set out in Chapters 1–4 as you progressed through your research. I have suggested that you prepare a *preliminary outline* (or a similar organizational tool, if you prefer) of the principal issues you intend to address before you start your search for primary authorities, and that you modify this outline as necessary as you proceed with your research. I have also suggested that you take thorough notes to memorialize your research path, that you keep copies of the important authorities you find, and that you "link" (i.e., map) the authorities to the various points of law in your outline. If you've done those things, then creating your final outline should just be a matter of refining your working outline.

If you have a complicated research problem, you might consider using a software application to assist you with the organization, if you have access to such a tool. Several commercial applications are available; Lexis' *CaseMap* is perhaps the best known. These tools are particularly helpful if your research is being incorporated into a complicated brief with a lot of evidentiary support, or if it is being used for trial preparation. Applications such as CaseMap allow you to quickly retrieve for any given point of law in your outline all the legal authorities, witnesses, documents, deposition cites, paragraphs from pleadings, etc., that support or relate to that point.

For most straightforward legal-research projects, however, a relatively simple outline should suffice. But you still want to make sure that you "link" your research results to the points in your outline. So under each point and sub-point in your outline, include citations to the cases and other authorities supporting that point, along with parenthetical descriptions of the case holdings.

Once you have created this type of detailed outline, your research project is basically complete, and you can proceed to prepare your ultimate work product (e.g., a legal memorandum, a brief, or an opinion letter). The final outline, together with your revised question presented and your short answer, should form the skeleton for the first draft of your ultimate work product. You may want to reorganize your work product a bit after the first draft, but that shouldn't be too difficult once you have a complete draft of your analysis on paper.

In sum, diligently following the five steps outlined in Chapters 1–5 will not only ensure that your research is accurate and thorough, it will also make it significantly easier for you to prepare your ultimate work product.

PART II

REFINING YOUR LEGAL RESEARCH SKILLS

■ ■ ■

The five-step strategy discussed in Part I provides a solid foundation upon which you can develop your research skills. But merely reading the proposed strategy will not automatically turn you into a first-rate legal researcher. You also need abundant practice in putting this strategy to work. And you need to develop good work habits as you begin to practice law. This part of the book outlines some important considerations you should keep in mind as you continue to develop and refine your legal research skills. Chapter 6 offers ten research tips to help summer associates and beginning lawyers succeed in the practice of law. And Chapter 7 addresses some common problems beginning lawyers encounter in their research, along with ways to overcome these problems.

CHAPTER 6

TEN TIPS FOR THE SUMMER ASSOCIATE AND THE BEGINNING LAWYER

■ ■ ■

A. Carry a Legal Pad
B. Keep the Lines of Communication Open
C. Don't Forget: Money Matters
D. Learn Your Way Around the Law Library
E. Keep Track of Where You've Been and Know Where You're Going
F. Don't Reinvent the Wheel
G. Remember That Annotations and Headnotes Are Not Cases
H. Find Answers, Not Just Authorities
I. If at First You Don't Succeed, Persist!
J. Don't Ignore Those Red Flags!

Learning how to do legal research in law school is one thing; applying that learning in the workplace is another. Expectations are different in the employment setting, and there are things you need to know that you won't learn in law school. This chapter discusses some important considerations law students and beginning lawyers should keep in mind as they make the transition from law school to the practice of law. It is based in large part on interviews I conducted with numerous lawyers from a variety of backgrounds and levels of experience regarding their advice for beginning lawyers on legal research. You can save yourself a lot of aggravation if you take these tips to heart early in your career.

A. CARRY A LEGAL PAD

Waiting in my office for my two supervisors to come by for my first-ever annual review was, as you might expect, a bit nerve-racking. I *thought* things had gone well that first year. My supervisors had *seemed* happy enough with my work. But since I had never had a law-firm performance review previously, I wasn't quite sure what to expect. And after all, this was one of Washington, D.C.'s biggest law firms, and the expectations would be high. What if they didn't think I was smart enough? What if they didn't think I knew enough about the law? What if they didn't think I was a good enough writer—or *researcher*, for that matter? What if . . . well, you know the feeling.

When my supervisors showed up smiling and laughing, the "what-ifs" went away. And thankfully, to my relief, the review went quite well. My supervisors focused mainly on the positive, rather than on my rough first-year-lawyer edges. In fact, the main thing they wanted me to work on was not my smarts, my knowledge, or my writing, but rather my *note-taking*, or more properly, my lack thereof. Specifically, one of the partners found it quite annoying that I would come by his office to receive an assignment, but I would not write down what he said during the meeting. (Apparently I erroneously thought I had a good memory for detail.) Then I would return a few days later for clarification, and still not write down what he said. Then finally, on my third visit, he would look annoyed, pull out a legal pad, toss it in front of me, and tell me to make sure that I wrote it down this time. In the end, he was pleased with my work product, but my poor note-taking habits caused my supervisor some unnecessary irritation.

And so it is in the working world: often, it's not a beginning lawyer's lack of ability that causes problems, but rather a lack of attention to the little things. So take a lesson from my experience: always carry a notepad (or its electronic equivalent) when you meet with people. Pay close attention to what your supervisor says when you receive an assignment, and make sure that you record it accurately. Of course, you don't want to get so caught up in note-taking that you fail to grasp the significance of what your supervisor is saying. But you also don't want to pester your supervisor later with follow-up questions about matters that were discussed in your initial meeting. Good note-taking (which means listening carefully while still recording the essence of what someone tells you) is an important skill that will serve you well throughout your career.

B. KEEP THE LINES OF COMMUNICATION OPEN

In addition to taking good notes during your meetings with a supervising attorney, you should strive to maintain good communication with your supervisor as you proceed with your research project. If you are unclear about something that is discussed during the initial meeting, ask for clarification. The best time to ask questions is while you are there in the first instance. You want to make sure that you understand the assignment fully and that you know exactly what type of work product your supervisor wants you to produce. And don't hesitate to ask the supervising attorney for more background information about the case or the transaction if you feel it would help you to understand the research assignment more fully.

Furthermore, you should return to your supervisor for guidance if your research doesn't go as planned, or if you need further information in order to find an answer to your research problem. You should also return to your supervisor if your research turns up some new leads that look promising and you think perhaps you should explore a different angle from that which you previously discussed with your supervisor. The important thing is to keep the lines of communication open as you proceed with your research assignment. Research can take unexpected turns, and you need to maintain a meeting of the minds with your supervisor so that you don't go off on an unhelpful tangent. This is particularly important if you cannot find any useful authorities on point and you are not sure whether to keep searching or to make do with what you have (see Chapter 7, section D). Your supervisor is in the best position to judge whether the extra expenditure of time and money is justified in a particular instance; in addition, your supervisor may have some helpful ideas for further research that you hadn't considered.

In the end, you need to balance the risk of annoying your supervisor with too many pesky questions against the risk that you will get off track and turn in a poor work product if you remain silent. And the latter is definitely the greater of the potential evils. In my first-year evaluation, I still got a very good review, notwithstanding my poor note-taking. But I have no doubt that my review would have been significantly less favorable had I simply guessed at what my supervisor wanted, and as a result turned in an unhelpful work product. So don't be afraid to ask your supervisor questions about your research assignment, both in your initial meeting and as you proceed—just make sure to write down the answers.

C. DON'T FORGET: MONEY MATTERS

In law school, because you are not charged for your use of WestlawNext, Lexis Advance, or Bloomberg Law, it is easy to get in the habit of relying on these commercial services freely without concern for their cost. But in the practice of law there may be times, as discussed further in the next section of this chapter, when you will instead want to do library research, or use free or less-expensive internet resources, in order to cut costs. (*See also* Chapter 7, section B, for more on the choice between library research and online research.) Depending on the client, the commercial service you choose, and the nature of the project, the expense of using an online commercial service may not be justified in a particular situation.

On the other hand, while beginning researchers often think of electronic research as expensive, there are times when it is more efficient, and therefore cheaper in terms of the overall cost to the client, to use an online commercial service. If, for example, you bill your client for the time it takes you to trudge down the block to the closest law library to look at a case in print, instead of quickly pulling up the case using a commercial service, you are likely to cost your client money. And the same is true if you waste an hour of billable time looking at a free internet resource such as Wikipedia, when you could have found the answer in 15 minutes by using a good secondary source on WestlawNext. So part of being a good researcher is developing an awareness of cost considerations—including the cost of your time—and thinking about the balance of costs and efficiencies while you research.

One important aspect of this cost consciousness is an understanding that not all research projects are created equal when it comes to resource consumption. Your client's financial resources and the importance of the particular research project to the overall case will influence how much time you spend on a project and the type of research tool you should use. A corporation involved in bet-the-company litigation may want your firm to leave no stone unturned when it comes to a particular project, while an individual or small-business client looking for some quick advice on a relatively mundane transactional matter probably does not want you to prepare a research tome in response to its questions. Make sure you talk to your supervisor regarding every project to see roughly how much time your supervisor thinks you should spend on it (*see also* Chapter 7, section C), and when in doubt, verify whether you are free to use online commercial services, and if so, which ones.

I once asked a summer associate to research a relatively straightforward issue while I was away at a trial one day, assuming it would take him only an hour or so in the library. When I came back, he had the answer and gave me a short memo summarizing his research. I thought nothing more about it until the computer-research bill showed up on the client's preliminary invoice later that month, and there I saw a computer charge for several thousand dollars for that one small project. Apparently the summer associate ran one fruitless search after another for hours before finally stumbling upon a search that worked. And since the summer associate had chosen transactional billing over hourly billing (*see* the discussion below), he was able to ring up a huge fee in a relatively short period of time for work that probably could have been done for free in the library. Needless to say, my client was not thrilled with the news, and the firm ended up eating a significant portion of the charge.

Fortunately, given the way law firms are now billed for electronic research services, these types of unpleasant situations are much less common. Still, it is important to attain a basic familiarity with the costs of the services you use.

First, you should be aware that different commercial services charge significantly different rates. Until recently, most students coming out of law school were familiar with only the two largest providers: Westlaw and Lexis. But Bloomberg Law is now a significant player as well, particularly in the area of corporate and transactional law. And many law schools are now providing training on Bloomberg Law in addition to training on WestlawNext and Lexis Advance.

There are other, lesser-known online services available as well, including *Loislaw* (which is affiliated with Wolters Kluwer, the parent of Aspen Publishing), *Versus law*, *Casemaker*, and *Fastcase*. The latter two in particular (Casemaker and Fastcase) are now widely used by practicing lawyers, since local bar associations frequently provide one of them for free to their members as a membership benefit.

While the lower-cost services may not have all the same capabilities and coverage as WestlawNext, Lexis Advance, or Bloomberg Law, their more competitive pricing makes them attractive in certain contexts. If you are researching a complicated problem on behalf of a large corporate client, for example, it might make sense to use WestlawNext, whereas if you are researching a relatively straightforward matter on behalf of an individual client, it might be better to use Fastcase or one of the other less-expensive services, particularly if you are just looking for primary authorities.

Google Scholar (www.scholar.google.com) can also come in handy when you're trying to cut costs. This service offers free access to cases, as well as law review articles and books. It can serve as a useful starting point for your case-law research when you're trying to hold down expenses. Just remember that you will need to use a citator to validate the cases, as well as to expand and update your research after you have found some initial cases (*see* Chapter 4).

You should also be aware that the commercial services have alternative types of billing arrangements. Traditionally, with classic Westlaw and Lexis, you had to choose whether you wanted to be charged by the transaction (for example, by each search), or by the amount of time you spent using the service. For any given project, the option you chose would depend upon factors, such as the number of searches you anticipated executing, and the amount of time you thought it would take to review the responsive materials.

These days, however, most firms pay a flat monthly subscription fee that varies by the number of lawyers using the service, the type of content included in the plan, etc. Most firms then prorate the charge to clients on whose behalf the services are used. Thus, as long as you stay within the subscription package, it doesn't matter how much you research, the firm pays the same fee, though your client may end up being billed for a greater portion of it. But if you access documents outside of the firm's subscription package, the firm will incur an additional fee.

Keep in mind that there are also free internet alternatives to fee-based electronic research services. Government agencies, courts, certain law schools, and other organizations make various sources (generally primary sources rather than secondary sources) available on their websites, which you can access free of charge. Some of the more important of these organizations are the following: *Justia* (www.justia. com), the Cornell Law School's *Legal Information Institute* (www.law.cornell.edu), *American Law Sources*

On-Line (www.lawsource.com), *Google Scholar* (www. scholar.google.com), and *FindLaw* (http://www.findlaw. com). For federal materials, the United States Government Publishing Office's *FDsys* website has a comprehensive, free collection of primary sources.

Just be aware that free resources may not be as comprehensive or up-to-date as fee-based services, and that your ability to search within the sources may be limited. Still for cost-sensitive research projects, they can be quite helpful.

There are also some significant new fee-based online services that have either recently gone to market or are expected to become available in the near future. Wolters Kluwer is rolling out a new product called *Cheetah* that it claims will combine high-end performance with ease-of-use at a competitive price. And a fairly new venture, *Ravel Law* (www.ravellaw.com), offers a novel way to analyze research results, relying on data visualization tools to show the researcher at a glance how significant cases are and how they relate to one another. Cases are represented on the screen as circles of varying sizes and colors; leading cases appear as larger circles. And when you run the cursor over the various circles, the lines connecting them demonstrate the relationships between a given case and the other cases.

Probably the most significant new product on the research horizon, however, is a service called *Ross*. Built upon *Watson*, IBM's cognitive computer, Ross is designed to function as an artificially intelligent attorney, providing meaningful answers to legal research questions framed in natural-language, rather than just providing research results. If it works as IBM hopes, Ross could be a real game-changer, reducing the amount of time lawyers spend analyzing research results, and thereby making the legal research process much simpler and more efficient. Time will tell whether this proves to be the case.

Finally, in order to become more cost-conscious about your research, I would consider keeping a *time log*, with fairly detailed descriptions of your research for each research project you work on, even while you are in law school and still learning how to do research. This is a good habit to develop early on, since your employer will likely require you to keep such records once you start practicing. It also encourages efficiency because it helps you keep in the forefront of your mind how much of your time and your client's money you are spending on a given research project.

While it may not be apparent in law school, money and time matter a great deal in the practice of law, particularly in private practice. The more cost-conscious you become in law school, starting with your research habits, the better prepared you will be for the realities of legal practice.

D. LEARN YOUR WAY AROUND THE LAW LIBRARY

It may seem hard to believe, but there was a time—not all that long ago, really—when computer research didn't exist. Back in those forlorn days, lawyers had to rely on books alone for their legal research, which often forced them to leave the comfortable confines of their offices and trek through the office, or perhaps even to another building, to do their research in a law library. There young lawyers would while away the hours with their heads buried in treatises, reporters, and numerous print volumes of the Shepard's citator.

Today, of course, things are different, and lawyers do most of their research online, either in their offices or in some other convenient location. So it is easy to forget the important role the library played, until quite recently, in the practice of law. And likewise, it is easy for the beginning researcher to see the law library as little more than a historical relic.

But even if you are an avid devotee of electronic research, you should familiarize yourself with library research and develop a basic competence in using print resources as well as electronic resources. Electronic research services and the internet have revolutionized legal research, and they are invaluable tools. But there are still some good reasons why you need to know your way around a law library if you want to be a first-rate researcher.

The first reason is that law libraries are still important for finding certain legal sources. While the principal online commercial services contain a wealth of information in their databases, they have not yet compiled *everything* you will ever need to research. Some resources you may still need to research in print. This includes not just obscure resources, but also some more commonly used tools, such as certain specialized treatises and practice manuals, as well as loose-leaf services, that you may come to rely on frequently if you practice in a heavily regulated area of law, such as tax or employee benefits. (*See* Chapter 6, section F, and Chapter 8, sections B, F, for more on specialized research materials.) And as discussed below, even when these materials are available online, it is sometimes easier to use them in print.

Furthermore, your particular employer may have limited access to online commercial research services, or may not want you to use them on certain projects that are cost-sensitive. As discussed in the previous section of this chapter, the principal online commercial services can be expensive, and it is not that uncommon, even in a larger law firm, for your supervisor to ask you to limit use of them on a particular project. So it is good to familiarize yourself with library research (as well as free internet resources) in case you need to rely on it for a cost-sensitive project.

A further benefit of law libraries is that they are the domain of law librarians—and a good law librarian can be a researcher's best friend. For law students in particular, the assistance of the law school's professional library staff is an invaluable resource. If you are looking for an obscure source or you don't know where to look for a particular type of authority, a knowledgeable reference librarian can point you in the right direction. And when you are stuck in your research and don't know how to proceed, your law librarian, who has a wealth of knowledge about available resources, can often refer you to a helpful secondary source that will stimulate your thinking and get your research moving forward again. (For more tips on how to overcome confusion during a research problem, *see* Chapter 7, section F.)

One other good reason you should familiarize yourself with library research is that the printed page is sometimes easier to work with than the computer screen. For some types of sources (e.g., case reporters), it makes little differences whether you look at them online or in print. But with for some other types of online sources (e.g., loose-leaf services), you cannot readily scan the surrounding sections and jump back and forth between sections in order to put your research in context and see whether various sections are germane to your research. With a print copy, you can more easily flip through the various sections, the table of contents, and the general index to assure yourself that you've found everything on point.

For these reasons, it would be wise for you to practice using print sources on occasion, and to know how to make appropriate use of the important resources law libraries offer. (For more on the choice between library and computer research, *see* Chapter 7, section B.) You should also learn what types of resources are available in your particular law library, and where they are located.

E. KEEP TRACK OF WHERE YOU'VE BEEN AND KNOW WHERE YOU'RE GOING

It is very important when you research to maintain at all times a clear understanding of where you are in the research process, so that you don't lose track of what you have already done, and so that you don't lose sight of your ultimate goal. Think of this as the research equivalent of tracking your position with a GPS when you go for a hike in unfamiliar terrain.

First, you should keep good *records of your research* so that you'll know what you've already looked at as you proceed with your research, and you won't have to reinvent the wheel in the event you need to revisit an issue later. You should keep track of the various search terms and electronic word-searches you've employed, as well as the authorities you've analyzed, with brief notations as to why you decided to include or exclude each authority. The principal online commercial services make this easy by automatically recording your searches and your research trail, and by providing online *folders* where you can store your research results.

Second, you should update your preliminary outline as you proceed, so that it reflects your evolving understanding of the legal issues involved in your research project. Then, as you proceed with your research, add citations to the authorities that address each of the various points in your outline, along with brief summaries of the case holdings.

Suppose, for example, that you are researching whether your client is liable under the tort doctrine of intentional infliction of emotional distress ("IIED"), and you have a four-part outline: one section for each of the four elements of IIED (intent, outrageous conduct, causation, and severe distress). Your outline should reflect, for each of these four points, which of your authorities support or address that point. It is also a good idea to keep copies (either print or electronic) of the key authorities you decide to include in your research, and to make notations for each one indicating which point(s) in your outline it addresses. In this way you effectively "link" the authorities you find to the points in your outline.

Detailed record-keeping may sound onerous, but it's really fairly simple when you get the hang of it. And the relatively small investment of time you make will pay off on those occasions when your research doesn't go as expected and you need to re-trace your steps— particularly if you are working on a complicated project. Good record-keeping also makes your final organization at the end of your project easier. You will already have a fairly detailed working outline that links each point in your outline to the authorities that address that issue. Then you can fairly easily convert this working outline to a final outline, and the final outline to your ultimate work product (*see* Chapter 5, section B).

In addition to keeping good records as you proceed with your research, make sure that you keep an eye on your final work product throughout your project. It's easy to get side-tracked in legal research, so you need to keep focused on your question presented and consider at every step how what you are finding relates to that question. Your outline should help in this regard. When you analyze any given authority, think about how it fits into your outline, and how ultimately it will help you find an answer to your research problem.

F. DON'T REINVENT THE WHEEL

As discussed in Chapter 2, secondary sources are important for a number of reasons. They are particularly important if you are researching in a specialized area of law, such as tax law, employee benefits, or commercial bankruptcy litigation. In these types of areas, specialized secondary materials are almost an essential part of the practice.

There are several types of specialized materials available to the practitioner. These include: (1) *loose-leaf services*, published by companies such as BNA-Bloomberg or CCH, that compile a variety of primary and secondary materials in one set of volumes (*see* Chapter 8, section F); (2) multi-volume, *specialized practice manuals and treatises* that focus on narrow areas of law, such as federal-securities litigation or eminent domain; and (3) *specialized newsletters* that keep practitioners up to date on the latest developments in particular areas of the law. Some of these materials are jurisdiction-specific; others are general. A good law library will carry most of them. The principal online commercial services also carry many of these specialized materials. But certain specialized materials, including some loose-leaf services, are only available online via a subscription.

The main advantage of specialized materials is that they allow you to research in a narrow area of the law without having to consult multiple sources, and without having to waste time sifting through mounds of irrelevant information. Loose-leaf services are particularly valuable for this because they collect secondary materials and various types of primary materials in one place so that you don't have to look at multiple, often obscure sources to find what you are looking for. Essentially, they offer the researcher one-stop shopping.

When I first started practicing law in Washington, D.C., I worked in my firm's health-care department. A big part of the practice involved issues surrounding Medicare and Medicaid reimbursement. Probably the most important research tool I used (in addition to a multi-volume treatise on administrative law) was a loose-leaf service called the *CCH Medicare and Medicaid*

Guide. It contains both federal and state materials pertaining to the Medicare and Medicaid programs, including statutes, regulations, court decisions, agency decisions, and various other materials, as well as commentary explaining the primary authorities, and updates on recent activities in Congress and at the Department of Health & Human Services. Looking up all of these materials separately, even assuming I could have found them all, would have been a very time-consuming task. The loose-leaf service made it easy by putting them all in one set of binders.

So if you find yourself researching a specialized area of law, be sure to ask your supervisor or your reference librarian whether there are any loose-leaf services or other specialty materials that might facilitate your research. They can make your research a lot easier.

G. REMEMBER THAT ANNOTATIONS AND HEADNOTES ARE NOT CASES

This advice should go without saying, but my practicing-lawyer friends tell me it is still an issue for some beginning lawyers, so let's make it abundantly clear: *annotations* and *headnotes* are merely tools for finding cases, *not* case substitutes.

When I was a senior associate, my supervisor once asked me to work with a law-student intern on his writing. "It's really bad," he said. He wasn't kidding. When I looked at the (purported) memorandum the intern had turned in, I was amazed to see a two-page document consisting almost entirely of individual headnotes from various cases re-printed verbatim on the paper. He even included the headnote numbers. And that was it: there was no analysis or even factual discussion, just a vague conclusion like "and so the client will win" at the end of the headnotes. Needless to say, I knew I had my work cut out for me.

Now I don't expect that too many law students these days would turn in that kind of work product, given the increased focus on legal writing on the part of law schools. But you may at times be tempted to rely on an annotation to provide a supporting citation, without actually going to the trouble of looking up the actual case and reading it. And you may at times be tempted to review only the headnotes of a case to determine whether to include it in your research results—again, without reading the text of the case itself. But you should flee from such temptation. Annotations and headnotes should be limited to their intended use. Annotations are designed to help you make a first cut as to relevance. Once you have determined that the case may be on point, you need to read the actual opinion. Headnotes are designed to help you find where in cases certain discussions are located, and to help you find related cases. You should not rely on them to accurately summarize what is contained in the actual case. Instead, you should read the actual language of the decision to determine whether the case is germane to your research problem.

Trying to shortcut your research problem by using annotations and headnotes in inappropriate ways is unwise because you risk skewing your analysis with an incorrect reading of a case. Taking the little extra time required to read the actual decision is an inexpensive way to insure against this risk.

H.   FIND ANSWERS, NOT JUST AUTHORITIES

Beginning researchers sometimes have a tendency to want to canvass an entire area of law when they do research (even, on occasion, its historical development), instead of focusing their attention on the answers to specific research problems. This seems to stem from a fear that they might miss something if they don't look at all authorities that could even remotely bear on their issue. The problem with this approach is that you can get yourself into a quagmire; the further you go in looking at tangential issues, the harder it is to find your way out of the mess. Law is an interconnected web, and you will always find one more angle to look at if you don't keep your attention focused on solving your specific research problem.

As discussed in Chapter 4, there are better ways to make sure you are not missing important authorities than collecting every case that could possibly be relevant and then trying to sort through them all. (*See also* Chapter 7, sections H and I, for more on knowing how to end your research without fear of missing an important case.) It is important to be persistent and redundant in your research efforts if your initial searches are not productive (*see* section I below). But there is no reason to look at every case remotely connected to the general topic if your initial searches are productive and lead you to cases that are on point and factually similar to your research problem. Instead, you should follow the procedure set out in Chapter 4 for expanding and updating your research, which will automatically focus your follow-up research on the authorities that are most relevant to your specific research problem. Your goal is not to prepare a mini-treatise on an area of law, but to advance your client's interests with respect to a specific problem or opportunity.

I. IF AT FIRST YOU DON'T SUCCEED, PERSIST!

The flipside of researching too broadly, which was discussed in the previous section, is the tendency some beginning researchers have to give up too quickly when they don't find specific answers to their research questions right away. Sometimes you will find the answer to your research problem fairly easily; at other times, the answer can be quite elusive. And sometimes you will discover after thorough research that there simply is no clear answer.

No matter how methodical you are in following the research strategy set out in Chapters 1–5, there is no precise formula for solving research problems. Every problem is a little different because the facts of any two cases are invariably different, and you generally cannot predict with any great degree of confidence exactly how your research is going to turn out. And while you do not want to waste your client's money spinning your wheels, you sometimes need to try different approaches and be redundant in your efforts to locate relevant authorities when you cannot find anything directly on point. (*See* Chapter 7, section D, for more on what you should do if you cannot find any controlling cases on point.)

One time a business owner hired me to handle an appellate matter before the 10th Circuit Court of Appeals. The company wanted to appeal a summary-judgment order that the trial court had entered against it in a contract dispute. I asked an associate to help me research the opening brief, and after several days of evaluating the facts and researching the law, he reported back to me that the client had no chance of winning on appeal and should not even bother pursuing it. I thanked him for his hard work and asked him to dig a little deeper. The associate came back a second time and told me that his follow-up research confirmed his original assessment—that any such appeal would be futile. At that point I explained that the client was paying us a lot of money to make the best arguments we could, and that he really needed to try to find *some* kind of authority to support our position before we just threw in the towel. I suggested some additional avenues to explore and sent the associate back to the library.

My third meeting with the associate was the charm. It turned out that the law was not nearly as unfavorable to our client as the associate had originally thought, particularly in light of the vague language of the controlling contract. Using the new research he found (i.e., a couple of persuasive cases from another state), we were able to craft a good argument that the contractual language was ambiguous on a key point and should be construed in favor of our client, since the other company had drafted the agreement. The court agreed with this argument and reversed the summary-judgment order that the trial court had entered against our client.

Stories like this one underscore the importance of not rushing to the conclusion that there are no authorities on point when you research an issue, particularly when the stakes are high. And they remind me of what a curmudgeonly lawyer I once knew used to tell young lawyers that worked for him: "I didn't hire you to tell me how to lose the case. I can do that myself. Just tell me what I need to know in order to win!"

You don't always need to have a controlling authority on point. Sometimes you can find helpful persuasive authorities to use when there are no controlling authorities on point, and sometimes you can argue by analogy to related areas of law. (*See* Chapter 7, section G, for more on using persuasive authorities.) Think creatively: constructing a legal argument is as much an art as it is a science. And keep open the lines of communication with your supervisor when your research doesn't go as planned. Your supervisor is in a better position than you to judge whether a given project merits additional research and may well have some good advice on different approaches to try. (*See also* Chapter 7, section H for help on knowing when to end your research.) Just keep mind that it is the trait of persistence that frequently separates the first-rate researcher from the average researcher.

J. DON'T IGNORE THOSE RED FLAGS!

There is one final bit of advice that *should* go without saying, but I would be remiss if I did not say it again: you absolutely *must* validate the authorities you rely on (using a citator) before you turn in your final work product. There are no exceptions to this rule.

Failing to validate your authorities is a serious omission that can get you in big trouble. Once, when I was an associate, my firm had an important, emergency hearing in federal court in a case that was well-publicized by the local media. A small team of us put together a lengthy brief in a short time frame, and it was filed with the judge the afternoon before the hearing. The next day, just as the hearing was about to begin, a young lawyer who was in charge of researching a portion of the brief announced frantically that he had discovered an error in his research. It turns out that one of the main cases we were basing our argument on in the brief was no longer valid because it relied upon a statute that had subsequently been repealed. Had the young associate validated the statute before turning in his research, as he should have, he would have seen that the statute had been repealed. But apparently he didn't realize that statutes need to be validated, just as cases do. As a result, someone had to take a note to our lead lawyer—while he was in the hearing—informing him that he could not rely on this case, which was one of the cornerstones of our argument. Suffice it to say, it was not a happy day for the young associate.

So make sure you validate (using Shepard's, KeyCite, or BCite) all of your statutes, cases, and regulations before you rely on your research results. And that means more than just making sure that there are no red flags (or comparable symbols) next to an authority. Sometimes you can still use a case even though the citator displays a red flag, since the part of the holding that is invalidated may not be relevant to your factual scenario. (Of course, other things being equal, you would prefer a precedent that was not partially invalidated, but that may not always be possible.) Conversely, even the presence of a yellow flag can sometimes indicate that you should not rely on an authority. A case you want to rely on, for example, may be distinguished by a controlling authority on factual grounds that are on par with your factual scenario. So you need to make sure you read and analyze each case or other authority with a red or yellow flag next to it before you conclude that it is a reliable authority.

If you are not sure whether you validated your authorities earlier in your research, or if any significant amount of time has passed since you last did it, then you should validate them again to be on the safe side. The peace of mind you buy will be well worth the small additional outlay of time and money. (For more on using citators, *see* Chapter 8, section H(2).)

CHAPTER 7

TROUBLE-SHOOTING GUIDE

■ ■ ■

A. "I'm Not Sure How to Get Started on My Research Project."

B. "I Don't Know Whether I Should Research a Given Project in the Library or Online."

C. "I Don't Know How Much Time I Should Devote to a Given Project."

D. "I'm Not Finding Any Authorities on Point."

E. "My Electronic Word-Searches Are Yielding Too Many Cases to Sort Through Efficiently."

F. "I'm Half-Way Through My Research Project and I'm Really Starting to Feel Confused."

G. "I'm Not Confident in How to Use Persuasive Authorities."

   1. When to Use Persuasive Authorities

   2. Which Persuasive Authorities to Use

   3. How to Find Persuasive Cases

H. "I'm Not Sure When or How I Should End My Research."

I. "I'm Afraid That I Might Have Missed an Important Authority."

J. "I Don't Know How to Organize the Results of My Research for My Final Work Product."

K. "I Don't Know Which Cases are the 'Best' Cases to Use."

Sometimes, even the best legal researchers encounter problems. The five-step strategy discussed in Chapters 1–5 will help you find solutions to legal research problems efficiently and accurately, but it will not immunize you completely from the types of frustrations every legal researcher deals with from time to time. This section discusses some of the more common obstacles you may expect to encounter, and the ways to get around them. The choice of topics is based primarily upon reports from law students and beginning lawyers as to the types of problems that they have encountered in their research efforts.

A. "I'M NOT SURE HOW TO GET STARTED ON MY RESEARCH PROJECT."

To begin with, if you haven't read the first chapter of this book, you'll want to do so. As that chapter discusses at length, you need to develop a *research plan* at the beginning of your project. Before you begin looking for authorities that address your research problem, you should think carefully about the precise *question(s)* you need to answer and the *research path* that you think will lead you to that answer. You'll also need to think carefully about which *search terms* and *electronic word-searches* will best enable you to access the various sources of law.

Assuming you have followed **Step 1** carefully and are still unsure where to begin, it is likely that you either: (1) are unsure what exactly you are supposed to be looking for, or (2) do not know enough about the particular area of law you are researching to make a reasonable assessment as to the types of authorities that are likely to control the analysis.

The first problem—not being confident in what you are looking for—often arises because you do not have a meeting of minds with the supervisor who gave you the assignment. Perhaps your supervisor was very busy at the time you met and didn't have time to explain a project in depth. Or perhaps you got nervous because you were working with a particular senior lawyer for the first time, and this nervousness interfered with your listening comprehension. In any event, you always want to be on the same page with your supervisor on what exactly you are supposed to be researching. If you feel uncertain during your initial meeting as to the nature of the assignment, make sure you ask clarifying questions at that time. It is natural to avoid such questions for fear of appearing ignorant, but the downsides of turning in a poor work product far outweigh this concern.

Furthermore, you shouldn't be afraid to go back to your supervisor in the middle of your research project if you have lingering doubts about the direction of your research. You don't want to go overboard and make yourself a pest, or ask the same questions repeatedly (remember, take notes!), but seasoned lawyers understand that summer associates and beginning lawyers may need a little guidance as they proceed with a project. Maintaining good communication with your supervisor as you progress through your research can save you a lot of time and needless stress (*see also* Chapter 6, section B).

The second problem—not knowing enough about an area of law to know where to look for authorities—can be resolved by obtaining some additional background information about your specific problem and about the area of law you have been assigned to research.

First, it is helpful to review some of the important documents in the *client file*, such as the pleadings and briefs in a litigation matter, or the agreements and correspondence in a transactional matter. The factual background you obtain will help to put your research issue into context.

Second, in order to gain general background information on an unfamiliar area of law, you should consult one or more *secondary sources*. A brief review of an appropriate secondary source can help you frame your research problem and separate out tangential issues. Often the key to gaining clarity on your research assignment is simply to analyze carefully how your precise question presented differs from related legal questions. Reviewing secondary sources before you begin your search for primary authorities will help you frame your question presented within its broader legal context. (*See* Chapter 2, section A, for more on using secondary sources to obtain background information on a topic.)

Finally, you should not hesitate to talk with colleagues if you feel uncertain about a research problem. If you have a real-estate problem and you have a friend in the firm who practices real-estate law, that person should be able to point you in the right direction. Furthermore, a colleague may be able to examine your research problem from a different angle or suggest an approach you hadn't thought about. And often the mere exercise of talking through a problem and explaining it to someone else can help you focus your own thoughts. So don't underestimate the importance of networking— even within your own firm, and even when you are just starting out in the practice of law. Fostering a few mutually supportive relationships can go a long way toward helping both you and your friends advance in your careers.

B. "I DON'T KNOW WHETHER I SHOULD RESEARCH A GIVEN PROJECT IN THE LIBRARY OR ONLINE."

The appropriate roles of online and library research were hotly debated when Westlaw and Lexis first came upon the legal scene several decades ago. It was apparent to everyone from the start that electronic research could save researchers significant time with certain tasks, so its value was pretty obvious. Yet there were also a lot of detractors in the early days who believed that, while computer research had its place, it should be limited to certain functions, such as pulling up cases and validating them. Some of that reticence, as you might expect, was based upon the natural reluctance some of us who have been around a while tend to have toward doing things differently from the way we've always done them. Some of it was based upon legitimate concerns about the limitations of Westlaw and Lexis in their early forms. And some of it was based upon cost considerations, as well as a legitimate concern that beginning researchers would rely too heavily on electronic word-searches, at the expense of secondary sources and such. (Of course, the latter argument is not a legitimate reason to steer beginning lawyers away from computer research *per se*. It is merely a reason to stress to them the importance of following a sound research strategy, such as the one set out in Chapters 1–5 of this book, so that they don't rely exclusively for their research on electronic word-searches.)

The situation today, of course, is quite different. As lawyers trained on electronic research have assumed their places in the upper echelons of the legal system, the resistance to technological change has greatly ebbed. Additionally, the online commercial services have made significant strides in expanding their coverage and improving their capabilities since the early days, so a lot of the legitimate early criticism is now moot.

The advent of the internet has also had a big impact. A lawyer can now do computer research at home, in the office, or in another part of the world, whereas the original Westlaw and Lexis terminals were confined to captive law-library cubicles. Furthermore, in recent years there has been a proliferation of free legal material available on the internet that could only be found in law libraries in the early days of computer research. And there are now a number of online commercial services besides Westlaw and Lexis that generally offer lower prices (though also less-comprehensive services in many cases). (For more on the differences between commercial online-research services, *see* Chapter 6, section C.)

So electronic research is now the default option, and the only remaining question is whether, on a given project, there is some reason you would want or need to do your research using print sources in a library, rather than looking at electronic sources on a computer. There are still some resources that are available only in print (e.g., certain treatises and specialized practice manuals), and this will likely remain the case for the near future at least. Furthermore, many researchers find it more convenient to review certain types of sources (e.g., loose-leaf services) in print rather than online. (For more on the virtues of library research, *see* Chapter 6, section D.) But for the most part, online research is quicker and more convenient. Therefore, as long as you have access to it, and it is cost-efficient (balancing the cost of the online service against the time savings), you should feel free to use your computer for as much of your research as you can. Remember, however, that if you have any doubts about the cost-efficiency of a given project, you should discuss the issue with your supervisor before you start your research. (For more on the cost considerations affecting legal research, *see* Chapter 6, section C.)

On the other hand, if you prefer library research, that is generally fine as well. There are definitely times when you should *not* do your research in print sources because it is inefficient to do so. If, for example, you have to walk several blocks to look at a resource in a library that you could look up right away on a free online site, it is hardly reasonable to pursue the print source. But normally, the choice between computer research and library research comes down to a matter of balancing convenience, cost, and personal preference. So if you work for an employer that has a substantial law library, and you prefer to read A.L.R.'s articles in print instead of online, by all means enjoy your time in the library. In fact, there are sometimes advantages to being a little "old school" in life, and it may just warm the heart of that (super) senior partner down the hall to see you enjoying yourself in the firm's law library instead of gazing at the ubiquitous computer screen. After all, many large firms made big investments in their libraries, and it is desirable to let the partners see that their hard-earned money is still going to good use.

Regardless of your personal preference for books or computers, however, you should become skilled at using both. Certainly the expectation today is that a beginning lawyer will be highly proficient at online research, and you can advance your career by pursuing advanced electronic research training, and by otherwise honing your electronic research skills. But it also pays to know your way around a law library (*see* Chapter 6, section D). So even if you have a decided preference for electronic research, you should also become proficient at using print sources if you want to be a first-rate researcher.

C. "I DON'T KNOW HOW MUCH TIME I SHOULD DEVOTE TO A GIVEN PROJECT."

This is a common problem for newer lawyers. In law school, you always had a definite deadline for your projects; in practice, you may not. But if you don't have a strict deadline, how do you know if you are putting too much time into a research project, or not enough?

To a large extent, this turns on the importance of the project. If you are just looking for an authority to support a peripheral point in a brief, you obviously do not want to spend as much time turning over every stone in search of the perfect case as you would if you were researching the decisive issue in the litigation.

Your reasonable expectations based on your background knowledge of the law should also guide you. If you are quite sure that an area of law (say, for example, a tort action for false imprisonment), is governed by case law rather than statutory law, you would probably be justified in undertaking only a cursory search of the state code, just to make sure there were no statutes on point. But if you are quite sure there is a state statute that addresses the issue, then you should keep digging, even if you do not find anything on point right away. For this reason, it is important to educate yourself broadly about the topic through secondary sources so that you understand the basic legal framework before you start looking for authorities. (For more on using secondary sources to obtain background information on an area of law, *see* Chapter 2, section A.)

It is also important, when you are a newer lawyer especially, to keep your supervisor apprised of your efforts. There is nothing wrong with asking at the beginning of the project how much time the supervisor anticipates that the project should take. The supervisor may say that you should just take a quick look at something, or that you should spend no more than a few hours researching an area of law. Don't disregard these directions. Lawyers don't like it when they ask an associate to take a quick look at an issue, and then they see when examining the billings at the end of the month that it took the associate 50 billable hours to complete the task. Make sure that you have some idea of the supervisor's expectations regarding time at the beginning of the project, and check back with a progress report if the project seems to be taking longer than expected.

Finally, assuming you keep in mind the considerations discussed above, the short answer to how much time you should spend on a given project is this: as much time as you need to finish the project. That, of course, raises a further question: how do you know when you are properly finished with your research? That issue is discussed below in section H of this chapter.

D. "I'M NOT FINDING ANY AUTHORITIES ON POINT."

Sometimes the reason beginning researchers can't find any controlling authorities on point is that there simply aren't any. But more often it is because: (1) they are confused about the law and are looking for authorities in the wrong places; (2) their search terms and/or electronic word-searches are inadequate; or (3) they are not extrapolating broadly enough from their research results. So, before you stop researching and conclude that there are no authorities on point, you need to make sure that you've addressed these three possibilities.

You first want to make sure you understand the basic legal framework of your problem and give some thought to where you are likely to find controlling authorities. For this it is helpful to go back to secondary sources to place your legal topic in its larger context. You should be able to tell from your review of secondary sources what types of authorities are likely to control the analysis, and where you are likely to find them.

Suppose, for example, that your client owns a shopping center and wants to know whether the shopping center is legally prohibited from leasing space to a gun retailer. If you start searching for federal cases to see whether there are any legal restrictions on the ability of shopping centers to lease space to gun retailers, you are likely to come up empty because any restrictions of this type are likely to be found at the local level, not at the federal level. No matter how good your search terms and electronic word-searches are, your searches will be unsuccessful because you are searching in the wrong source. What you should do is locate the applicable municipal code and the local zoning regulations and review their restrictions on commercial leasing. (*See* Chapter 9, section G, for more on researching local law.) A good secondary source, such as a treatise on commercial real estate, can re-focus your research and ensure that you are looking in the right places for relevant primary authorities. (For more on using secondary sources to re-focus your research, *see* Chapter 2, section E.)

A second reason why lawyers sometimes have trouble finding any controlling authorities on point is that their search terms and/or their electronic word-searches are too narrow. The solution in that event, of course, is to try formulating some additional searches. If you are researching in print, you may need to use broader search terms, or to think of broader concepts and synonyms when you access tables of contents or indexes. If you are researching online using electronic word-searches, you can broaden your searches by using broader search terms, fewer search terms, and less-restrictive terms and connectors. (For more on how to improve your search terms and your electronic word-searches, *see* Chapter 1, section B.) You can also try running a topical search if you have only been using electronic word-searches, and vice versa. Terms-and-connectors searches, in particular, can be tricky for the beginning researcher. On the one hand, they allow you to home in on issues with great precision. But on the other hand, they can miss relevant authorities if you do not craft them properly, so a topical search can serve as a check on the reliability of your electronic word-searches. Thus, if you are having trouble finding cases with one tool, you should try the other.

Third, before you conclude that there are no controlling authorities, give some thought to whether the authorities you did find are more on point than you may have assumed. Beginning researchers sometimes make the mistake of thinking that there are no authorities on point because the authorities they have found are not precisely on par factually with their research scenarios, or do not precisely address their question presented. But often this just means that they need to *extrapolate* a bit from the existing authorities to arrive at a reasonable conclusion. You won't often find a case with precisely your fact pattern, but that doesn't necessarily mean that a case isn't on point. You may need to think a little more creatively to answer your question(s) presented, taking rules out of their specific factual contexts and applying them in a new or broader context.

To paraphrase a hypothetical the well-known legal philosopher H.L.A. Hart once posed, suppose a certain municipality passes a very basic ordinance: "No vehicles are allowed in Washington Park." Your client wants to operate his vintage moped in the park. You've found three previous decisions on point: one holds that *cars* are "vehicles" within the meaning of the ordinance; one holds that *motorcycles* are "vehicles" within the meaning of the ordinance; and one holds that *bicycles* are **not** "vehicles" within the meaning of the ordinance. So based on the available law, is a *moped* a "vehicle" within the meaning of the ordinance? Your authorities will not give you a definitive answer to this question because there is no authority precisely on point. So you will need to creatively analyze the authorities you found to determine what you think the likely outcome would be if your client's case were to proceed to litigation. Is a moped operating with its engine on more like a car/motorcycle, or more like a bicycle? What if the operator is merely peddling the moped with the engine off? Does the legal status of a moped change depending on whether the engine is running or not?

As long as you have been careful in your research and have followed the steps set out in this book, you should not feel befuddled because you cannot find a case that fits your precise factual situation. Lawyers get paid not just to find the law, but to analyze it and apply it as well. Sometimes you will need to think creatively about the existing authorities you've found and use your best judgment to determine how you think a court would (or should) apply them in your situation. Beginning researchers sometimes find the indefiniteness of the law disconcerting, but in time you will become comfortable with the occasional absence of clear answers to your research problems. This doesn't mean you haven't done a good job on your research; it just means that you can't easily separate legal research from legal analysis.

Finally, if you have addressed all three of the potential pitfalls discussed above, and you still can't find any controlling authorities on point, you will probably want to look for *persuasive authorities* to fill in the void. In fact, you may want to look for persuasive authorities even if you *do* find cases from the controlling jurisdiction that are roughly on point, if, as discussed above, you find it necessary to extrapolate from those cases to reach your conclusion. In that event, finding a case from another jurisdiction that is more on par factually with your research scenario than the cases from the controlling jurisdiction will help to buttress your conclusion. (*See* section G of this chapter for more on how to find and use persuasive authorities.)

Again, it is always a good idea to discuss with your supervisor how much additional effort you should devote to a given project before you get too deep into a search for persuasive authorities. But as a rule you should err on the side of persistence when it comes to legal research (*see* Chapter 6, section I). Spending a little more time on your research than you planned is preferable to coming up empty-handed when there are relevant authorities to be had.

E. "MY ELECTRONIC WORD-SEARCHES ARE YIELDING TOO MANY CASES TO SORT THROUGH EFFICIENTLY."

Sometimes, the problem with using online electronic word-searches is not that you cannot find *any* authorities, but that your searches yield *too many* authorities. This makes your research inefficient because you waste time sifting through a lot of irrelevant search results. There are several steps you can take to address this problem.

First, if you are executing natural-language searches online, you normally want to filter cases by *relevance* (i.e., depth), as opposed to date or some other variable. The newer search engines are pretty good at prioritizing the most important authorities, so take advantage of the technology. Also make sure that you are searching within as narrow a database as possible. You don't want to search through all federal cases in the Ninth Circuit if you know you need a case from the U.S. District Court for the Southern District of California.

Second, you should revisit your question presented and make sure that it is not too broad. Are you framing the question narrowly, so that it addresses precisely what you are looking for, or is it a vague, general question? If your question presented is overly broad, your search terms are likely to be overly broad as well. Perhaps you need to be more specific about the factual context of your research problem. You can also use more precise terminology in framing the question presented: try "schnauzer," for example, instead of "dog," or "draft" instead of "negotiable instrument." You may also want to revisit secondary sources to borrow some of the specific terms of art they employ in discussing the subject matter. (For more on using secondary sources to refine your search terms, *see* Chapter 2, section B.) Once your question presented is more narrowly framed, then the search terms you derive from the question presented should become more precise as well. (For more on narrowing the scope of your search terms, *see* Chapter 1, section B(1).)

Finally, if you are still having problems with the broadness of your electronic word-searches, even after you have taken these steps, then the problem is likely due to the manner in which you have combined your search terms into electronic word-searches. So you will need to work on formulating more narrowly crafted word-searches. If you have been using *natural-language* searches, you should consider using *terms-and-connectors* searches as well, since these give you the ability to formulate very precise searches. (For more on narrowing the scope of your electronic word-searches, *see* Chapter 1, section B(2).)

An alternative way to deal with the problem of too many search results is to use a *topical search* (i.e., subject-matter search) in addition to electronic word-searches. This allows you to start with a broad topic in the index and then look for successively narrower topics until you find a manageable number of annotations. If you are researching on WestlawNext or Lexis Advance, you can use their online digest functions (e.g., the West Key Number System) to search by topic, drilling down to successively narrower topics until you get to a manageable level of specificity. If the most specific topic is still too broad, you can enter your own key words to narrow the results even further, though usually the most specific sub-topics (at least within a particular jurisdiction) have a manageable number of corresponding annotations. (For more on using digests and topical searches, *see* Chapter 8, section H(1).)

F. "I'M HALF-WAY THROUGH MY RESEARCH PROJECT AND I'M REALLY STARTING TO FEEL CONFUSED."

For the legal researcher, there are few things more frustrating than investing a significant amount of time in a research project, only to feel more uncertain about the solution to the problem than you were at the beginning of the project. But don't worry: it happens to all of us from time to time. You just need to relax, take a few deep breaths, and reassess the situation.

Generally this problem arises when researchers haven't really figured out the nuances of their research problem yet, leading them to conflate issues that are closely related, but subtly different. Often this is because they don't understand the *context* of their research well enough. If you don't know enough about the general subject matter, then you are more likely to get confused by the nuances. To remedy this, you first need to gain a better understanding of the broader topic and think about how your topic relates to other topics that are similar, yet different.

One good way to gain a better understanding of the context of your research is to go back to *secondary sources* for an overview of the general topic (*see* Chapter 2, section E). As you are doing so, think about how your specific issue fits into a larger legal category, and how it is distinguishable from the other topics in that category. Consider also sketching an outline or a chart that shows how your specific issue fits within the structure of the larger topic. Getting a clearer understanding of the logical relationships between your specific topic and other related topics should help to alleviate your confusion.

Suppose, for example, that you are researching the litigation doctrine of *collateral estoppel,* which is also known as *issue preclusion*. You need to know whether your client, who is the defendant in a lawsuit, is precluded from challenging an adverse factual determination that a judge made in an earlier case involving your client. If you are not conversant with the law governing the preclusive effects of earlier litigation, you may become confused by cases applying similar but subtly different doctrines, such as *equitable estoppel* and *claim preclusion*. And you may become further confused by cases discussing *res judicata,* which is sometimes used as a general term encompassing both claim preclusion and issue preclusion, but other times is used as a synonym for claim preclusion alone. By reviewing a good secondary source on civil procedure, such as *Moore's Federal Practice* treatise, and analyzing how these similar concepts relate to one another and how they differ, you can reduce your chances of going off on research tangents that ultimately have no bearing on your problem.

Often the reason researchers confuse related issues that arise in the course of their research projects is that they fail to adequately think through the nuances of their problems at the beginning of their research. It is important to analyze your research problem and plan your research *before* you start looking for primary authorities. (For more on formulating a research plan, *see* Chapter 1, section A.) If you don't, you risk confusion in the middle of your project because your broad pursuit of related topics will often get you further and further from the answer you need as you follow up on each tangential question that arises.

So if you start feeling confused in the middle of a project, you should, in addition to revisiting secondary sources, revisit your *question presented* and your *preliminary outline* to make sure that they are as precise as possible and don't conflate related concepts. Try to figure out how your question presented differs from related questions that look at first blush to be on point, but end up leading you away from your actual topic, and refine the language so that you eliminate any ambiguity. Consider also how the facts that are peculiar to your research problem distinguish your research scenario from some of the tangential cases you will read. Once you get clear on your precise question presented, then your search terms, which flow from the question presented, should automatically become more focused. And this improved focus should help you home in more accurately on relevant primary authorities.

Finally, there are some common-sense things you can do when you feel confused in the middle of a research project. Often you just need to take a break and do something else to let your brain relax. When you come back to it later, you'll probably find that you see the problem more clearly. It also helps to talk through the problem with a colleague, or perhaps with a research librarian. Not only might that person have some ideas you haven't thought of, but sometimes just explaining the problem to someone else—even without significant input from the person you are talking with—can help you work through the obstacles that have been holding you back.

So when you start to feel confused, relax and remind yourself that what you are experiencing is common. Legal research is complicated, and it sometimes yields no clear results. Learning to live with a bit of uncertainty is just part of becoming a seasoned researcher.

G. "I'M NOT CONFIDENT IN HOW TO USE PERSUASIVE AUTHORITIES."

Beginning lawyers are often uncertain about the role of *persuasive authorities* in their research. (Persuasive authorities, as you recall, are authorities, such as cases from other states, that are not controlling on a court, but merely provide guidance as to the appropriate way to decide a case.) It is sometimes difficult to know *when* you should rely on persuasive authorities, *which* persuasive authorities you should rely on, or *how* you should go about finding them. This section addresses each of those concerns.

1. WHEN TO USE PERSUASIVE AUTHORITIES

Most often, lawyers turn to persuasive authority when the controlling law in a jurisdiction is unclear. Usually this is because courts in the controlling jurisdiction have simply not had the opportunity to consider the specific legal issue.

However, there may be other reasons why the law is not clear. For example, there may be a precedent in the controlling jurisdiction that is roughly on point, but it is not very close on the facts to the case at issue. If there is a case in another jurisdiction that is closer on the facts, you can reasonably argue that a court in the controlling jurisdiction would likely have reached a similar result as the out-of-state case if it had been confronted with similar facts. In that specific factual context, you can argue, the law of the controlling state is unclear, and the reviewing court should look to the out-of-state precedent for guidance.

Another reason the law in a particular jurisdiction may be unclear is that there are conflicting decisions in the controlling jurisdiction, and it isn't clear how the cases can be harmonized. For example, there may be decisions from two different appeals-court panels that reach contrary results, and you cannot easily synthesize a rule from them that would apply to your case. In that scenario, you may want to look to out-of-state cases or even a secondary source for guidance in choosing between the conflicting rules. (For more on dealing with conflicting cases, *see* Chapter 5, section A(2)(b).)

Furthermore, on occasion, lawyers may use persuasive authority to argue against the law in the controlling jurisdiction, even though the existing law is relatively clear. For example, it might be worth arguing in an appeal to a state supreme court that the leading authority in the jurisdiction on a point of law, a decision from the intermediary court of appeals, should be overruled (or at least disregarded) because it is contrary to the majority rule in all or most other jurisdictions, and it is a poorly reasoned decision. To support that type of argument, you would want to cite well-reasoned cases from other jurisdictions (and perhaps also certain secondary sources) that are contrary to the controlling precedent.

Depending on the situation, therefore, persuasive authorities can fill a gap in the controlling law, add greater specificity to the controlling law, or even serve as a basis for challenging the controlling law. Accordingly, if your research fails to turn up any controlling authorities directly on point, you would *generally* want to look for persuasive authorities to fill the void, particularly if your case is one of first impression in the controlling jurisdiction. (Before you spend a lot of time looking for persuasive authorities, however, you should check with your supervisor to make sure that you are both on the same page with respect to the additional time expenditure.)

2. WHICH PERSUASIVE AUTHORITIES TO USE

Once you have decided to look for persuasive authorities to buttress your research, you will need to decide *which* persuasive authorities to rely on. Most often, when lawyers think of persuasive authority, they think of cases from outside the controlling jurisdiction. But there are other types of persuasive authority as well.

If your research involves statutory interpretation, for example, you may at times want to rely on the commentary to a *model code* provision for persuasive authority, if the language of the model code tracks the language of the controlling statute in question. Furthermore, you can sometimes look to how the courts in a given jurisdiction have interpreted the language of a non-controlling statute that has similar language, in order to shed light on how the controlling statute should be interpreted.

Suppose, once again, that your research involves the meaning of the term "motor vehicle," but this time in a state statute prohibiting the operation of motor vehicles in state parks. If you cannot find a case on point, you may want to look at how the term "motor vehicle" is defined elsewhere in that state's code. Perhaps there is a separate statute that prohibits the driving of motor vehicles while intoxicated, and there is a case that interprets the term "motor vehicle" for purposes of that statute. (Or perhaps the non-controlling statute has a definition section that includes the term.) In that scenario, you can look to the way "motor vehicle" has been interpreted (or defined) with respect to the non-controlling statute for guidance in construing the same term in the controlling statute. (Note that the same applies for *regulations* and *ordinances*: if a certain term has been defined or interpreted with respect to a non-controlling provision, you can look to that definition or interpretation for guidance in construing the same term in a different provision in the regulatory or municipal code.)

But most often, it is cases from outside the controlling jurisdiction that lawyers turn to for persuasive authority. If you are researching a matter of *federal law*, you will want to look to decisions from federal courts of appeals and federal district courts outside the controlling circuit. If you are researching a matter of *state law*, you should start by looking for federal cases from the applicable district and circuit that interpret the controlling state's law. While not themselves controlling, federal cases interpreting state substantive law are considered highly persuasive in the absence of contrary decisions from the state's own appellate courts. And if you cannot find any decisions from the federal courts interpreting the state's law, then you will want to look at cases from other states to see if they have addressed the issue. Typically, this will be in the context of state common-law issues. Occasionally, however, you might cite an out-of-state case to support a statutory interpretation argument, if the statutory language in question is sufficiently similar to that of the controlling jurisdiction (e.g., where both statutes are based upon a model code, such as the Uniform Commercial Code).

Keep in mind that not all persuasive cases are of equal weight. A supreme-court decision from another state, for example, is going to carry more weight (other things being equal) than an intermediary court-of-appeals decision from that same state. Likewise, a case that is close on the facts to your case will carry more weight than a comparable case that is factually inapposite. The age of the case will also factor in: generally, the newer the case, the more authoritative it is. And a case supported by sound, detailed reasoning that has been cited frequently by other cases is going to be more authoritative than a short, conclusory opinion that has garnered little attention.

Some judges even take into account the jurisdiction from which the persuasive case arises, and the stature of the judge who wrote the majority opinion. For example, a judge in the controlling state may find cases from neighboring states more persuasive than cases from other parts of the country. The justice I clerked for on the Michigan Supreme Court, conversely, favored decisions from the New York and Massachusetts high courts because of their long-standing, well-developed jurisprudence, and because they had produced some very highly esteemed jurists over the years, such as Benjamin Cardozo and Oliver Wendell Holmes.

The procedural posture of your case will also affect what decisions are most persuasive. For example, if you are before a federal *district court* in the Eighth Circuit, that court may regard decisions from other district courts within the Eighth Circuit as more persuasive than the decisions of U.S. courts of appeals from outside the Eighth Circuit. On the other hand, if your case is on appeal to the Eighth Circuit, that court may regard the relevant decisions of the other U.S. courts of appeals to be more persuasive than the decisions of district courts within the Eighth Circuit.

So a number of factors can influence the weight a court will assign a particular persuasive case. You will need to consider them carefully when choosing which cases to use for your analysis. (For more on choosing which authorities to rely on in your analysis, *see* Chapter 5, section A(2)(a), and Chapter 7, section K.)

Finally, *secondary sources* can serve as persuasive authorities in certain circumstances. Most commonly, you would use a secondary source as a persuasive authority for one of two reasons. The first is to establish the majority rule on a particular point of law (but make sure the source is current). The second is to persuade a court that a certain position is better reasoned or more in keeping with a current trend in the law than an alternative position. On rare occasion, you might even need to rely on a secondary source as persuasive authority because there are not any controlling or even persuasive cases on point (e.g., in a new or rapidly changing area of law).

As with cases from other jurisdictions, secondary sources vary as to their authoritativeness when used as persuasive authorities. Courts give some of them, such as the Restatements and certain well-respected treatises, a significant amount of weight, while others, such as A.L.R.'s and legal encyclopedias, are not considered very authoritative. (*See* Chapter 2, section D, and Chapter 8 for more on using individual secondary sources as persuasive authorities.)

3. HOW TO FIND PERSUASIVE CASES

Finding persuasive cases basically involves the same process as finding cases from the controlling jurisdiction. (*See* Chapter 3, section C(3), for more on how to go about finding cases generally.)

First, you can revisit secondary sources to see if you can find a discussion of your issue; if so, they will likely refer you to at least some cases from various jurisdictions that have addressed the issue. An A.L.R. annotation is probably the most useful secondary source for this purpose, if you can locate one on point, since A.L.R. annotations provide a plethora of case references to all the various jurisdictions. If you cannot locate an A.L.R. annotation on point, try a loose-leaf service, a multi-volume treatise, or the applicable Restatement. All of these secondary sources contain numerous citations to cases from a variety of jurisdictions.

Second, you can use West Publishing's *Key Number System* to look for cases in other jurisdictions by topic. If you have already found a case in the controlling jurisdiction that is roughly on point, but perhaps not quite factually on par, you can use the key number for the topic to find cases from other jurisdictions that may be closer factually to your research problem. If you do not already have a controlling case that is roughly on point, you can use the Key Number System to do a topical search, drilling down from broad categories to your specific topic. (*See* Chapter 4, section B, for more on using the Key Number System.)

The third—and probably the easiest—way to find persuasive cases on a certain topic is simply to run the same electronic word-searches you ran in your search for controlling authorities on that topic, only this time using a combined database. The online commercial services have various combined databases that allow you to search for all federal cases, all state cases, or combined federal and state cases. Simply select the appropriate database and run the same search. Assuming your search for cases in the controlling jurisdiction came up dry because of an absence of case law rather than a poorly structured word-search (*see* section D of this chapter if you are not sure), you should be able to quickly locate any cases on point from other jurisdictions. On the other hand, if you end up having to modify your original electronic word-search to find cases on point from other jurisdictions, make sure you try the successful, modified word-search in the controlling jurisdiction as well, just to make sure your failure to find controlling cases there was not the result of a defective electronic word-search.

Once you find persuasive cases that address your topic, you can use them both to predict what a court in the controlling jurisdiction would likely decide if confronted with your specific issue, and to influence the court's decision if the matter proceeds to litigation. Even though persuasive cases are not binding on the courts, respect for precedent runs deep in the judicial temperament.

H. "I'M NOT SURE WHEN OR HOW I SHOULD END MY RESEARCH."

Beginning researchers often feel uneasy about terminating their research because there are always additional stones that can be overturned when you are searching for legal authorities. Sometimes the end game will be determined for you—when, for example, your supervisor tells you to spend an hour looking at a particular topic and report back. But typically, you will have to develop a sense for when you have researched thoroughly enough to feel confident in your analysis without having to look further. Generally this takes a fair amount of research practice. But there are some steps you can take to hasten the process.

First, you need to get in the habit of doing thorough, efficient research. If you have followed the five steps set out in Chapters 1–5 of this book, you should feel confident that you have done everything you needed to do to find a solution to your research problem. If you haven't already done so, read Chapter 5, which deals with the steps you need to take to finalize your research.

Usually, what beginning lawyers mean when they say they don't know how to end their research is that they don't know if they should keep executing additional searches, looking for more or better authorities. The answer to that question depends in large part on how successful your existing searches have been. If, after a thorough search following **Steps 1–3**, you've successfully found primary authorities that directly answer your question(s) presented, then you can move on to **Step 4** (*see* Chapter 4) to expand and update your case research. You don't need to look for every case that could possibly relate to the topic (*see also* Chapter 6, section H).

Let's say, for example, that after a thorough search for primary authorities, you find one controlling case that directly answers your question presented. At that point, you should first review the precedents that are cited *within* the controlling case to see if any of them are on point. If so, then include them in your research results. Next, you might want to execute a *key-number search* within the controlling jurisdiction to make sure there were no other important cases on point that you missed. And finally, you would want to use a *citator* to see if there are any more recent cases on point that have cited the controlling case. (If so, then you would need to use a citator on them as well, along with any new cases they cite that are on point, and so on, until you run out of new cases.) The main goal of this drill is to see whether there are any later cases that distinguish the case you intend to rely on, or modify its reasoning. Once you have completed that process, you can generally feel pretty confident in moving on to **Step 5** to finalize your research.

If your searches have *not* been very successful in answering your question presented, it gets a little trickier knowing when to quit. As discussed in Chapter 6, section I, you want to be persistent and try different approaches if you are not finding any controlling authorities directly on point. But if you've done this, and each different approach keeps leading you back to the same legal rules and the same authorities, you can take that as a pretty reliable indication that you haven't overlooked any important cases. And if you then expand and update your case research as described in the previous paragraph, and the additional cases you find are even less relevant to your research problem than the cases you've already found, then that is further confirmation that there are no cases more directly on point, and that you haven't missed any significant cases. At that point, you can end your search for controlling cases and consider (in consultation with your supervisor) whether you want to continue your research by looking for *persuasive authorities*. (For more on deciding whether to search for persuasive authorities, *see* Chapter 5, section A(3), along with section G(1) of this chapter.)

I. "I'M AFRAID THAT I MIGHT HAVE MISSED AN IMPORTANT AUTHORITY."

Related to uncertainty regarding the appropriate end point for a given research project is concern about missing an important authority. Unfortunately, there are no guarantees in legal research. However, if you have followed the suggestions set out in Chapters 1–5 of this book, you shouldn't have a problem. The important things to keep in mind are that you need to be *thorough* in your research, and that you should stress *redundancy* if you have any concerns about the thoroughness of your research (*see* Chapter 6, section I). You also need to make sure that you properly *expand and update* your case research, as discussed in Chapter 4.

Being thorough in your research means taking the time to work through each of the steps discussed in Chapters 1–5. Admittedly, you may find an answer to a research problem more quickly if, for example, you don't take the time to think about a research plan, or if you skip the step of reviewing secondary sources. And to be sure, there may be occasions when you are forced by time constraints to abbreviate your normal research process. But it is at these times that you run the highest risk of missing something important, so unless you are facing a real time constraint, it is generally not worth running that risk.

It also helps to be *redundant* in your research. Look at more than one secondary source, for example, if you don't feel comfortable with the area of law you are researching. Check the A.L.R.'s, look for a law-review article, or try to find a relevant loose-leaf service. You can also be redundant in your search for primary authorities. Instead of relying solely on electronic word-searches to find relevant cases, try a topical search as well. If you take more than one approach to finding legal authorities, and they lead you to the same results, you can be pretty confident that you have not missed anything important.

Finally, you need to make sure that you properly expand and update your research, as discussed in the previous section and in Chapter 4. This is an important step that many law students skip. For example, you need to make sure that you've used a citator not only to validate your authorities, but also to check whether there are more recent cases on point. You need to do this for all of your cases that are on point, and you need to keep doing it with each new case you find that is on point until there are no more recent citing cases to look at. (*See* Chapter 4, section C, for more on using a citator to update and validate your research.)

In sum, while you can never be absolutely certain that your research is bullet-proof, if you are thorough in your research strategy, redundant in your approach when faced with uncertainty, and careful to expand and update your research, you can have a high degree of confidence that you have not missed any key authorities.

J. "I DON'T KNOW HOW TO ORGANIZE THE RESULTS OF MY RESEARCH FOR MY FINAL WORK PRODUCT."

It is important to organize your research results not only at the end of your project, but throughout the course of your research. Basically this involves undertaking two tasks early in your research process.

First, prepare a *preliminary outline* of the major issues after you have reviewed secondary sources in **Step 2**, and remember to revise this outline as you progress with your research. (For more on preparing and revising your preliminary outline, *see* Chapter 3, section A.)

Second, keep good *records* of your research as you progress, and remember to "link" each authority that you intend to rely on in your analysis to one or more of the points in your outline. (For more on how to do this, *see* Chapter 6, section E.)

If you do these two things, it should be fairly easy to finalize your outline after you have completed your research, and from there it should be relatively easy to prepare your final work product. (For more on finalizing your research, *see* Chapter 5, section B.)

K. "I DON'T KNOW WHICH CASES ARE THE 'BEST' CASES TO USE."

Frequently, your research will produce multiple cases that stand for roughly the same point of law. Deciding which (and how many) of these cases to use in your work product can be challenging, but there are some guiding principles to keep in mind.

First, as to how many cases you should cite, the short answer is: no more than necessary. Long string citations can be tedious for the reader, and they generally do not add much, unless the point of law is unsettled. On the other hand, it can sometimes be helpful to cite more than just one case on a point of law. If, for example, the leading case (defined below) is dated, you might want to include a newer case along with it to show that courts still follow the same principle. Or you might cite both a state supreme-court case that is only marginally on par with your case, together with a state court-of-appeals case that is closer on the facts. Citing both cases shows the reader that the principle of law has been adopted by the highest court in the state, and also that it has been applied in factual circumstances similar to your case. The point here is to be conservative and deliberate in your case selection: if you cite more than one case on a point of law, make sure you have a good reason for doing so.

Second, as for choosing among multiple cases that stand for the same point of law, the same factors that make one persuasive case "better" than another (*see* Chapter 7, section G(2)) apply with regard to controlling cases as well. First and foremost, you want to consider case hierarchy; that is, whether the case is from the controlling jurisdiction, and whether it is from the court of final resort or an intermediary appellate court. The other main factor you should consider is how closely the facts of your case match the facts of the precedent in question. If you can show that a rule of law has been applied in a factual context that is very close to your case, the precedent will be much more persuasive to the court.

Beyond these two main criteria, there are several lesser factors you should consider in choosing between cases that stand for roughly the same point of law. One of these is the age of the case. Legal principles evolve over time, so, other things being equal, a newer case is more likely to track the reasoning of the current court. Another factor is whether the holding of the case is significant with regard to the legal principle in question. This turns on whether it has been frequently followed by other cases (i.e., is a leading case), and whether it contains a clear, detailed analysis of the point of law in question. And finally, you may want to consider the reputation of the court, and of the judge who wrote the opinion, if you have access to that information.

In sum, deciding which cases to cite and how many cases to cite in support of a point of law cannot be determined mechanically. Rather, it requires a careful balancing of the factors discussed above, which can be daunting for a beginning researcher. In time, however, you will develop a better feel for it, as you refine your research skills further.

PART III

THE PRINCIPAL SOURCES OF LAW—AN OVERVIEW

∎ ∎ ∎

The principal focus of this book is on legal research *strategy*, rather than the process of researching individual sources of law. Nevertheless, it is important to understand how the various sources of law are organized, and how to access them. This part of the book thus provides a summary of the principal legal sources. For further reference, there are several helpful texts you can consult that go into greater detail on the individual sources of law, such as *Principles of Legal Research*, by Kent C. Olson, and *Where the Law Is: an Introduction to Advanced Legal Research*, by J.D.S. Armstrong and Christopher A. Knott. Check with your law librarian for additional recommendations.

Sources of law are conventionally catalogued into two groups: *secondary sources* and *primary sources*. Simply stated, secondary sources contain commentary about the law, whereas primary sources contain the law itself. Both are important to legal research. Chapter 8 summarizes secondary sources, and Chapter 9 summarizes primary sources.

Primary sources of law are available on all the commercial online services, as well as in print. Many of them are also available on free websites, such as the websites for *Justia* (www.justia.com), the Cornell Law School's *Legal Information Institute* (www.law.cornell.edu), *American Law Sources On-Line* (www.lawsource.com), *Google Scholar* (www.scholar.google.com), and *FindLaw* (www.findlaw.com). They are also available for free on some government websites, such as the

Government Publishing Office's *FDsys* website (www. gpo.gov), which makes available a number of primary sources that contain federal law.

The free online resources tend to be somewhat limited in their coverage. And they generally lack the sophisticated search capabilities of the principal commercial services. So you will probably not be able to rely on them exclusively for all of your legal-research needs. But they are nevertheless very helpful tools for the cost-conscious researcher. (For more on free and low-cost research tools, *see* Chapter 6, section C.)

The principal secondary sources, in particular, are proprietary, and therefore not available on free and low-cost sites. Outside of a law library, WestlawNext, Lexis Advance, and Bloomberg Law are your best bets for finding secondary sources. Remember, as discussed in Chapter 2, that you will normally want to consult one or more secondary sources before beginning your search for primary authorities.

CHAPTER 8

SECONDARY SOURCES OF LAW

■ ■ ■

A. Legal Encyclopedias
B. Treatises and Practice Manuals
C. Legal Periodicals
D. A.L.R.'s
E. Restatements of the Law
F. Loose-Leaf Services
G. Other Secondary Sources
H. Digests and Citators
    1. Digests
    2. Citators

Secondary sources are not themselves legal authorities. They are reference works designed to explain the law and to help researchers locate primary authorities. Related to these are *finding tools*, such as digests and case citators, which do not provide any background or commentary on the law but simply direct the user to primary sources of law. For the sake of convenience, digests and citators are summarized in this chapter along with secondary sources.

If you are researching in print, the various sources discussed below will likely be grouped together in one area of your law library. You can access them using the available indexes, tables of contents, or outlines for each source. If you are researching online, you can use these same tools, or you can use electronic word-searches.

As for which secondary source(s) to look at for a given project, the summary of sources below should help. It discusses what type of information each secondary source contains and what it is generally used for. As you become a more experienced researcher, you will see that certain secondary sources are better for some purposes than for others. When in doubt, look at more than one source, and if you don't find what you are looking for in one, try another. Also, even after you have started your search for primary authorities, you can easily circle back and look at additional secondary sources if your search for primary authorities is not going as anticipated.

The principal secondary sources and finding tools you are likely to use in the practice of law are discussed below. (For further discussion of the various uses of secondary sources, *see* Chapter 2.)

A. LEGAL ENCYCLOPEDIAS

Legal encyclopedias are like any other encyclopedia. They summarize the law by topic, and the topics are arranged alphabetically. They are perhaps the easiest of the secondary sources to use.

There are two main types of legal encyclopedias: one focuses on general legal principles common to most jurisdictions, while the other type is jurisdiction-specific. As for the former, there are two main general-law encyclopedias: American Jurisprudence 2d ("Am. Jur.") and Corpus Juris Secundum ("C.J.S."). As for jurisdiction-specific encyclopedias, a number of states have them (mostly the larger ones); they usually have names such as *California Jurisprudence*. These jurisdiction-specific encyclopedias are often more helpful than the general-law encyclopedias for identifying primary authorities, since they are more narrowly focused.

Encyclopedias are very accessible, and they can serve as a good starting point for research on an unfamiliar topic. If you have a broad topic, you may find it listed in the table of contents. If you have a more specific issue, you should use the topical index. Legal encyclopedias have extensive topical indexes arranged alphabetically, which you can access with your search terms (*see* Chapter 1, section B(1)). If you are researching online, you can also search for topics within the encyclopedia by using the table of contents and/or the index. You can also use electronic word-searches (*see* Chapter 1, section B(2)). Remember that you will need to check the pocket parts of individual volumes for updates if you are researching an encyclopedia in print form, just as you do for most other print sources.

Encyclopedias are useful for obtaining very basic background information on a topic, particularly in cases where you know little about the area of law and just need a broad overview. Generally, they do not provide detailed enough information to be more than a starting point for your secondary-source research, although they can sometimes be useful for finding primary authorities.

State-specific encyclopedias are helpful in that regard if you are researching an issue of state law.

Encyclopedias are not regarded as scholarly works, so they are not generally cited as persuasive authorities. Instead, you would want to cite a more authoritative secondary source, such as a Restatement or a multi-volume treatise.

B. TREATISES AND PRACTICE MANUALS

Treatises and practice manuals are reference works that summarize and provide information on individual areas of law. While there are no hard and fast distinctions between the two, most librarians use the term "treatises" to refer to more scholarly works that contain critical commentary and analysis, as well as background information, historical information, and references to primary materials. They have traditionally been written by law professors and are frequently contained in multi-volume collections. "Practice manuals" are similar to treatises, but as the name suggests, they have a more practical orientation. They focus on providing assistance to the practitioner in understanding and using the law, rather than generating scholarly commentary. Practice manuals can be either single-volume or multi-volume works. They are usually written by practitioners—sometimes by groups of practitioners that have different sub-specialties. The principal online commercial services carry a number of treatises and practice manuals.

Practice manuals are usually more specialized than treatises. Some of them (*state-specific practice manuals*) focus on the laws of particular states, while others (*specialized practice manuals*) are multi-jurisdictional, but have a narrow subject-matter focus (e.g., federal securities regulation or commercial-zoning law). Both types of practice manuals provide practical guidance and tips for practitioners, such as how to prepare various types of documents.

State-specific practice manuals (e.g., the *Rutter Group California Practice Guides*) are often very helpful if you are researching issues of state law because they provide background information on the specifics of state law, as well as citations to key primary authorities in the relevant state. Most states have a multi-volume, general practice guide; they usually have names such as the *Tennessee Practice Series*. Some of the larger states have additional specialized practice manuals as well, which focus on particular practice areas within a given state (e.g., *The Colorado Estate Planning Handbook*).

Practitioners in relatively arcane areas of the law have increasingly come to rely on specialized practice manuals, along with loose-leaf services (which are discussed in section F of this chapter), because they collect in one place various types of primary and secondary authorities relevant to the specialty, in addition to providing helpful background information about the primary authorities.

Treatises and practice manuals explain and analyze the law in significantly more detail than encyclopedias. Therefore, it is usually better to use a treatise or practice manual rather than an encyclopedia to learn about an area of the law, unless you just want a cursory overview of a general legal topic. Treatises and practice manuals are also helpful for finding primary authorities; this is particularly true of practice manuals because they are narrower in their focus.

Occasionally, treatises are useful as persuasive authorities (e.g., in situations where you cannot find primary authorities on point (*see* Chapter 2, section D)). This is particularly so when the treatises are complex, multi-volume works, when the authors are well-known and respected scholars, and when the treatises are kept up to date. Practice manuals are less frequently cited as persuasive authorities than multi-volume treatises because they generally lack critical commentary and analysis.

Treatises and practice manuals are easy to use. As with legal encyclopedias, you can use your search terms to access the topical index. Just remember that you may need to narrow or broaden those terms or look for synonyms (*see* Chapter 1, section B(1)) if you do not find what you are looking for in the index. If you are researching online, you can also use full-text electronic word-searches to customize your search. Lexis Advance and WestlawNext both carry good selections of treatises in their collections of secondary materials; Bloomberg is quickly assembling a significant collection as well. Be aware, however, that the three principal commercial services carry somewhat different collections, so if you cannot find a specific treatise on one service, you may need to check the other services too. If you are researching in print sources, check the subject index of your law library to see what is available.

Finally, when choosing a treatise, make sure that it is one that is updated regularly (most are), or it may no longer be reliable. Print versions are updated through soft-cover supplements and pocket parts. The online versions are updated automatically and should indicate the date through which they are current.

C. LEGAL PERIODICALS

Articles in legal periodicals can serve a similar function as treatises, providing detailed information about an area of law, but they are even more narrowly focused in terms of subject matter. They concern specific legal issues and do not attempt to canvas the whole of the law, as legal encyclopedias do, or even entire areas of the law, as treatises do. So depending on your topic, you may or may not find an article on point.

There are two main types of periodicals that are useful for legal research: *law-review articles* and *bar-journal articles*. The former are generally published by academic law reviews, and the latter by bar associations. Law-review articles are generally written by academics. They tend to be significantly more detailed than bar-journal articles, but they are sometimes too theoretical to meet the needs of practitioners. Bar-journal articles, on the other hand, which are generally written by practitioners, are more practical. For example, they may provide advice on how to draft a certain type of document, such as a non-competition agreement. But they are often too cursory to be very useful for in-depth legal research. Bar-journal articles are usually jurisdiction-specific, whereas law-review articles tend to focus on general legal principles. Thus, it is usually best to look for a state bar-journal article if you are researching a routine matter of state law, and to look for a law-review article if you have a complex or novel issue, or one that cuts across multiple jurisdictions.

Both bar-journal articles and law-review articles can provide useful background information on the topics they cover, as well as references to relevant primary authorities. In addition, a law-review article from a respected author that is right on point can make a useful persuasive authority, particularly in a new or unsettled area of law.

Legal-periodical articles are not difficult to find. Most articles that you would find useful for practical research are available through the principal online commercial services. You can find them either through topical indexes or through electronic word-searches, using the search terms that you generated in **Step 1** of your research (*see* Chapter 1, section B(1)). If you are researching in a library, you can use *LegalTrac,* the *Index to Legal Periodicals and Books,* or the *Current Index to Legal Periodicals* to locate articles in print form.

HeinOnline is another helpful resource that carries an extensive collection of law-review articles, along with a variety of other legal materials. It is an online subscription service, but most law libraries have access to it. HeinOnline is particularly useful when you are looking for older articles because its coverage of legal periodicals extends further back in time, making it a valuable resource for historical research.

Many law-review articles are also available online using free internet sources. If you know where an article is published and it is of fairly recent vintage, you can often access it for free on the applicable law review's website. If, on the other hand, you are searching for articles by topic, *Google Scholar* can be helpful for locating relevant articles, though it often refers you to fee-based services, such as HeinOnline, that require a subscription or a one-time payment if you want to download an article. You may also find some free law-review articles by simply using topical word-searches on Google.

One other internet resource that is very useful is the *Social Science Research Network*, or SSRN (www.ssrn .com). This online service provides a repository for scholarly articles (and drafts of articles) that may or may not be published elsewhere. Anyone can access them for free, and there are currently over 500,000 full-text papers in the repository, many of which are law-related. You can search for relevant articles on SSRN using electronic word-searches, or you can drill down through the topics in the online table of contents to find a desired topic.

Keep in mind that articles, unlike most secondary sources, are not updated, so you will need to consider whether a particular article is still timely before you rely on it, particularly if you plan to use it as a persuasive authority.

D. A.L.R.'S

American Law Reports is the name of a publication that has been around for nearly a century. It publishes "annotations," which (as the word is used in this context) are basically articles that summarize the case law across the country dealing with particular legal topics. Typically, an A.L.R. annotation will discuss one case in detail by way of example, and then briefly summarize other cases nationally that discuss the same issue. The cases are broken down by jurisdiction, and the annotation will generally try to distill a majority rule from the cases. A.L.R.'s are organized by series (e.g., A.L.R.1st, A.L.R.2d, etc.), with the first series containing the earliest annotations, and the highest-number series containing the most recent annotations. A.L.R.'s are continually updated with supplemental volumes, so even the earliest annotations will refer you to recent cases, unless, as occasionally happens, they have been superseded by later annotations. Separate series of annotations (A.L.R. Fed and A.L.R. Fed2d) are devoted to discussions of federal cases.

Both the print and online versions of the A.L.R.'s can be accessed through topical indexes. You can also run electronic word-searches, using the search terms you generated in **Step 1** to find annotations (*see* Chapter 1, section B(1)). In addition, the A.L.R.'s contain tables of authorities that allow you to search for annotations that discuss a particular case, statute, or regulation. And you may find a reference to a useful A.L.R. annotation in another secondary source, or through an online search for cases. Remember that if you are researching in print, you will need to check the supplements and pocket parts to find the most recent cases, and to make sure that the commentary is current.

There is no guarantee that you will find an annotation on any particular topic. But if you do find an annotation on point, it can often be quite valuable, both for providing an overview of the topic and the manner in which courts have addressed it, and for the detailed references it provides to primary authorities. A.L.R. annotations also contain a wealth of information on the other secondary sources available on a given topic. So if you have a complicated research topic, it is generally worth taking a quick look at the A.L.R.'s to see if there are any annotations on point.

A.L.R. annotations are not particularly authoritative when used as persuasive authorities, since they merely catalog cases and do not analyze legal trends or provide commentary. However, they are occasionally cited in briefs to establish what the majority rule is among the various states that have addressed a particular issue, where there is no more authoritative source on point, such as a Restatement or a multi-volume treatise. If you do decide to use an A.L.R. annotation for this purpose, make sure that the annotation is up to date.

E. RESTATEMENTS OF THE LAW

The Restatements of Law are compilations of rules, illustrations, and commentary that are prepared by the American Law Institute to organize and clarify the principles of the common law. They reflect the consensus of leading lawyers, judges, and academics who are considered experts in their respective fields.

The Restatements as a group are organized by subject matter (e.g., torts, trusts and estates, contracts), and there are three series: the original Restatements, the Restatements of the Law (Second), and the Restatements of the Law (Third). The third series is a continuing work in progress. The second and third series of Restatements include annotations (i.e., short summaries) of all the cases that have cited the various sections of the Restatements.

The individual Restatements are organized by section. Each Restatement has a topical index that allows you to find relevant sections using your search terms. You can also run electronic word-searches if you are researching online. Remember that if you are researching in print and are looking for case annotations in the appendices, you will need to check multiple volumes, each of which covers a different time period.

Each section of a Restatement discusses a particular point of law. Within each section, the governing Restatement *rule* is set out first in boldface. This rule is then followed by lettered *comments* that explain how the American Law Institute believes the rule should be interpreted. These comments generally include numbered, hypothetical *illustrations* (derived from real cases) that show how the rule applies in various factual settings. Next are *reporter's notes* and *cross-references* to relevant key numbers and A.L.R. annotations (*see* Chapter 4, section B, for more on key numbers). And last come *annotations* (i.e., short summaries) of the individual cases that have cited the Restatement rule; these annotations tend to occupy the bulk of any given section. Print versions of these annotations are mainly found in multi-volume appendices to the main Restatement volumes.

The Restatements are useful for obtaining background information about an area of law and the ongoing developments in that area. They also contain, mostly in the appendices, a treasure trove of case annotations, organized by jurisdiction. These summarize the cases that have followed the Restatement on a particular point of law. Thus, if the jurisdiction you are interested in has followed a particular Restatement rule, you can use cases from other jurisdictions that have followed the same Restatement rule as persuasive authorities in the controlling jurisdiction. (For more on using out-of-state cases as persuasive authorities, *see* Chapter 7, section G.)

Furthermore, a Restatement rule can itself serve as a persuasive authority in certain situations. Because they contain detailed analysis and are compiled by groups of highly respected lawyers, judges, and professors, the Restatements carry significant weight with the courts. Sometimes, in fact, state courts "adopt" sections of a Restatement, making those sections essentially the law of the state, and giving related sections, as well as the explanatory comments, significant persuasive authority. And even if the courts in a particular jurisdiction have not formally adopted a portion of a Restatement, they still tend to give the Restatements significant deference when the jurisdiction's case law is unclear.

Thus, if you are researching an area of law that is principally governed by decisional law, it is always good to see what the Restatement for that area of law has to say on the subject.

F. LOOSE-LEAF SERVICES

Loose-leaf services (also known as subject-matter services) are very useful tools, particularly if you work in a specialized area of law controlled by a complex statutory or regulatory scheme, such as tax law, workers compensation, ERISA, healthcare law, or securities regulation. Traditionally, loose-leaf services were multi-volume publications that were published on three-ring binders (hence the name).

Loose-leaf services gather in one place a variety of materials (such as statutes, regulations, legislative history materials, cases, commentary, and news items) pertaining to a particular specialty of law. Thus, loose-leaf services provide a sort of one-stop shopping tool for research in a specialized area of law.

Print versions of loose-leaf services (also called "inter-filed loose-leaf services") are still popular, due to their ease of use. They are updated regularly with replacement pages that keep the subscriber abreast of recent developments in the law. Most of these services are now available online as well, directly from the publishers, on a subscription basis. And a number of them are also available on WestlawNext, Lexis Advance, and Bloomberg Law, including loose-leafs from the two best-known publishers of loose-leaf materials, *CCH* and *BNA.* WestlawNext and Lexis Advance carry CCH publications, and Bloomberg Law owns BNA, which is now called *Bloomberg BNA.* If you are looking for a loose-leaf service on a particular subject, and you don't know if one exists, a publication called *Legal Loose-leafs: Electronic and Print* (Arlene L. Eis, ed.) is helpful. Or, if you are researching online, just check the list of publications available from the online commercial services.

By collecting all sorts of relevant materials in one set of volumes, loose-leaf services make the research process easier for specialists. They are expensive, but they can also be big timesavers. In fact, many specialized practitioners consider them indispensable research aids. (For more on using loose-leaf services, *see* Chapter 6, section F.)

Specialized legal newsletters are a related type of secondary source. Published on a daily or weekly basis, they keep practitioners abreast of current developments in specialized areas of law, such as banking law, or healthcare law. The commercial online services carry a number of these newsletters as well. One of the best known is *United States Law Week,* published by Bloomberg BNA, which provides regular updates on activities of the United States Supreme Court. If you are looking for a legal newsletter on a particular subject, check whether your library has a publication called

Legal Newsletters: Electronic and Print (Arlene L. Eis, ed.), which is a comprehensive guide to specialized legal newsletters.

G. OTHER SECONDARY SOURCES

There are other miscellaneous secondary materials besides those discussed above that you may occasionally want to consult when you undertake a research problem. This section provides a brief overview of the most important ones.

At the beginning of a research project, *hornbooks* and *nutshells* can sometimes be helpful, particularly if you just need some quick background information on a legal topic. These books are similar to treatises and practice manuals, but they are generally shorter and more basic, providing a general overview of the important topics in a particular area of law. They provide a good alternative to legal encyclopedias as a starting point for your research. Additionally, for state-law research, the Carolina Academic Press publishes state-specific research guides (e.g., Mark E. Wojcik's *Illinois Legal Research*) that provide helpful overviews of the research resources available in particular states.

Another good overview tool is the *50-state survey*. WestlawNext and Lexis Advance both offer this service. It basically gives you an overview of how each of the various states approaches a particular area of law governed by statute or regulation. It also provides citations and links to the individual state statutes or regulations on point.

In matters of statutory interpretation, *attorney general opinions* are helpful (and can make good persuasive authorities) because courts tend to give them significant deference in determining how to construe statutes. This is true both at the state and federal levels. You can find attorney general opinions online using the principal online commercial services, or at the websites for the individual attorneys general.

Uniform acts (such as the *Uniform Commercial Code*) and *model codes* (such as the *Model Penal Code*) provide another useful tool in areas of law governed primarily by statute. They influence statutory law in the same way that the Restatements influence the common law. Thus, if a certain state has adopted a model code, you can use case law from other jurisdictions that have adopted the model code as persuasive authority to interpret the meaning of the statutory language in question.

Another secondary source that can sometimes be useful in statutory research is a publication called *Words and Phrases*, which is published by West Publishing. *Words and Phrases* provides helpful references to cases that construe certain legal terms of art. More precisely, it catalogues in alphabetical order the headnotes from various cases in which the courts have interpreted key legal terms. Thus, it is a helpful tool if you have a legal dispute that turns primarily upon the meaning of a term or concept, as in the case of a statute that contains an ambiguous term.

In the litigation arena, there are two additional research tools lawyers frequently rely upon: (1) *pattern jury instructions*, and (2) *jury verdict reports*.

Judges use *pattern jury instructions* as templates when they fashion instructions for a jury. Judges are not limited to these pattern instructions, and they may supplement them with special jury instructions that are tailored to the particular case. But since pattern jury instructions have already been approved by the court system in a particular jurisdiction as accurately representing the law regarding a particular cause of action, defense, etc., they form the core instructions for most jury trials. As a result, they can be quite useful as research tools, particularly if you need to draft a complaint, because they set out the essential elements of the various causes of action and the defenses. Furthermore, they include citations to cases that support the language of a given instruction, so they are also helpful for finding leading cases on point. Pattern jury instructions are published for each jurisdiction in print form, and the principal commercial services also carry them online.

Jury verdict reports compile information about numerous jury trial outcomes and sort them by jurisdiction and cause of action. Most importantly, they provide realistic data about verdict trends, and also the amount of each award. Lawyers have traditionally used jury verdict reports to evaluate the likely outcomes of prospective lawsuits, and to value existing claims for purposes of settlement. Like pattern jury instructions, jury verdict reports are available in print, and they are also carried by the online commercial services.

In addition, WestlawNext and Lexis Advance now provide online tools (*Case Evaluator* on WestlawNext, and *Verdict & Settlement Analyzer* on Lexis Advance) that employ data analytics tools to apply the information gleaned from jury verdict reports to individual cases. Thus, you can filter by jurisdiction, cause of action, type of injury, judge, etc., to see for a particular type of case what percentage of such cases ended in verdicts, how often the plaintiff prevailed, what the average award was, and so on. This makes it significantly easier for lawyers to glean information from previous cases to use in case assessment.

You should also keep in mind the value of using other lawyers' work-product when you research an area of law. Traditionally, many law firms maintained brief banks (containing hard copies of actual briefs, motions, and memoranda the firm's attorneys had prepared on various topics), as well as forms files (containing samples of various transactional documents the firm's attorneys had created) to assist junior lawyers in preparing their work-product. These days, it is pretty easy to find such documents on your employer's network with a quick electronic word-search, even if your employer does not maintain a formal collection of forms and sample briefs.

In addition, there are other commercially available collections of forms, both for litigation documents (e.g., *American Jurisprudence Pleading and Practice Forms Annotated*) and transactional documents (*American Jurisprudence Legal Forms 2d*). The online commercial services carry extensive collections of these types of materials as well.

Sample documents are helpful because they can give you a head start on your project. Sample briefs and motions, for example, can be useful for litigation research because they provide citations to authorities that govern a specific area of law, and they also provide analyses of the law. Just remember that you still need to do your own research, even if you find a brief or motion on point. No two factual scenarios are exactly the same, so you cannot just adopt the analysis of a sample brief and apply it uncritically to your own research problem.

Keep in mind also that, depending on who wrote them, sample briefs and motions may not be as dependable as traditional secondary sources in describing the law. For one thing, they are not periodically updated, as are many traditional secondary materials. And their analysis will not generally be as objective as secondary sources because they are written in a manner favorable to a particular client's position. Nevertheless, as long as you take heed of these caveats, sample briefs and motions can make useful research tools.

The online commercial services also now carry some very helpful instructional materials geared toward the practice of law. These are particularly valuable for newer lawyers and for lawyers who are unfamiliar with a particular area of law. WestlawNext, for example, has recently introduced *Practical Law* (available from the main directory), which provides practice overviews, practice notes, sample forms, sample clauses, checklists, toolkits, updates, and practice pointers for a variety of different transactional and litigation topics (e.g., how to draft an employment agreement, or how to handle an employment litigation matter). The materials are prepared by respected practitioners from a number of different legal specialties who have been retained to offer practical guidance as to how to handle certain legal tasks. Lexis Advance has a similar product called *Lexis Practice Advisor*, which is accessible from the drop-down menu on the home page. And while Bloomberg Law doesn't have a directly comparable product, its *Practice Centers* (available from the main directory) contain a number of helpful resources, including *Practice Tools* (e.g., checklists) for a variety of different practice areas. Moreover, Bloomberg Law makes available an excellent collection of sample contract terms and clauses through its *Dealmaker Documents and Clauses* service. And its *Draft Analyzer* tool is very helpful for drafting transactional documents.

There are other miscellaneous sources of commentary and secondary materials besides those discussed above you may sometimes want to consult when you undertake a research problem. Legal newspapers and magazines, law firm and law library websites, government and other directories, CLE materials, advisory opinions, legal dictionaries: these are just some of the other sources of secondary material you may find useful in the practice of law from time to time.

In addition, you may occasionally need to engage in non-legal research. For example, you may need to find information about a corporation or other business, or you may want to browse through the current business news for a particular industry. WestlawNext, Lexis Advance, and Bloomberg Law all have extensive collections of these materials. Bloomberg Law is especially strong in this area, as their principal focus is on business law and business information.

Remember, if you have a difficult time researching a problem and are unsure what secondary sources are out there, a reference librarian can provide invaluable assistance.

H. DIGESTS AND CITATORS

Strictly speaking, digests and case citators are not secondary sources because they do not contain commentary on the law. But like secondary sources, they have traditionally served as aids for both finding and expanding/updating case research. (*See* Chapter 4 for more on expanding and updating case research.) Citators are also invaluable tools for *validating* authorities (i.e., for making sure that the cases, statutes, and regulations you want to rely on are still good law). (For more on the importance of validating the authorities you rely on, *see* Chapter 6, section J.)

1. DIGESTS

Digests are basically collections of short case abstracts, or "annotations," that are arranged alphabetically by subject matter. While they are mainly useful as finding tools, you can also learn a fair amount about an area of law by simply scanning the annotations on a given topic in the appropriate digest. West publishes a digest for each individual state, as well as *regional digests* that compile state-court decisions by area of the country. It also publishes *West's Federal*

Practice Digest for federal cases, and a combined digest of all state and federal cases called *West's General Digest.* (Note that the General Digest is non-cumulative, so in order to find earlier cases, you will need to supplement it with *West's Decennial Digests,* which summarize cases by 10-year periods.)

Once considered the "gold standard" for case research, digests remain a viable alternative to online electronic word-searches for locating cases, particularly if you do not have access to an online commercial service. While digests *per se* are found only in print form, WestlawNext, Lexis Advance, and Bloomberg Law all have online digest functionality that allows you to search for cases by topic (i.e., subject matter). Of these three services, WestlawNext is the most comprehensive, since it is able to take advantage of West's well-developed *Key Number System* to facilitate topical searches.

There are advantages and disadvantages to using topical searches rather than electronic word-searches to find cases. These days, most researchers prefer to use electronic word-searches for most of their research. For important or difficult research, however, I recommend that you search for cases both ways in order to minimize your risk of missing an important case.

To find cases in the print version of a digest, it is generally easiest to use the topical index. The topical indexes in the West digest system are called *Descriptive Word Indexes.* An alternative method is to search the general outline of major topics alphabetically for your broad topic, then look at the listings under that broad topic to find your precise topic. If you are not familiar with the subject matter, though, this may be less efficient than using the Descriptive Word Index. To access the Descriptive Word Index, start with the search terms that you generated under **Step 1**. But remember that you may have to modify your search terms to encompass broader or narrower concepts if you do not find what you are looking for with your initial search terms. (For more on modifying your search terms, *see* Chapter 1, section B(1), and Chapter 2, section B.)

West Publishing's Key Number System organizes the law alphabetically into more than 400 major topics, and these are then divided into more and more specific sub-topics until the sub-topics are reduced to individual points of law, each of which is assigned its own unique "key number." There are over 100,000 unique key numbers, and these key numbers correspond to the points of law found in the headnotes of individual cases. (Key numbers are easily identified by the little symbol of a key next to the topic and number.) You can start from the list of broad topics and drill down through a series of progressively narrower subtopics until you find the precise point of law you are looking for. You can also add your own search terms to narrow the list of subtopics if you are researching online.

One of the principal benefits of using the Key Number System is that once you have a case on point, you can use the key number corresponding to that point of law to find other cases on point, either within the same jurisdiction or in other jurisdictions.

Suppose, for example, that during your review of secondary sources on contract illegality under New York law, you found a North Carolina case that is right on point for your research project. By using the key number that corresponds to that point of law in the headnotes of the North Carolina case, you can easily find New York cases on the same issue (if there are any) by just looking up that key number in the New York Digest. And if you are researching on WestlawNext, this is even easier because you can just click on the key number you are interested in, and then select the jurisdiction(s) you want from a list. (For more on using key numbers to expand your case research, *see* Chapter 4, section B.)

As noted above, you can also search for cases by topic on Lexis Advance. To do so, click on the *Browse Topics* tab at the top of the main Lexis Advance page, then click on the *Topics* link. From there, choose your topic and subtopic from the list provided. Like WestlawNext, Lexis Advance also allows you to customize your searches by adding your own descriptive terms to narrow the scope of the existing categories.

Bloomberg Law's search-by topic functionality is more limited in scope, at least at this time. To search by topic on Bloomberg Law, go to the *Litigation & Dockets* tab, then click on the link for *Bloomberg BNA Outlines & Headnotes*. This feature lists certain broad topics, which are then broken down into narrower topics. Each of these is then classified by a unique number, rather similar to the West Key Number System.

If you are researching a digest in print form, remember that you will need to check the supplements and pocket parts in order to find the most recent case annotations on the designated topic.

2. CITATORS

Citators have been crucial research tools for generations of legal researchers. The two basic purposes of citators are: (1) to *validate* authorities (i.e., to check whether a particular case, statute, or regulation has been repealed, overruled, distinguished, etc.), and 2) to find for a given case, statute, or regulation, all of the cases (and other materials) that have cited that authority. The first function (as discussed in Chapter 6, section J), is essential for making sure your authorities are still good law before you rely on them. And the second function (as discussed in Chapter 4, section C), is important for *updating* your case research.

Each of the main online commercial services has its own citator. The original citator service was *Shepard's*. It is now owned by Lexis and is available on Lexis

Advance. WestlawNext has its own citator called *KeyCite*. And Bloomberg Law has its own citator called *BCite*.

When it comes to *case validation*, case citators are very user-friendly. When you pull up a case or other authority, you will see a red or yellow/orange symbol if there has been any "negative treatment" by one or more later cases. You can then click on a link to examine the negative treatment in more detail (click on the *Negative Treatment* link, for example, if you are using KeyCite, to see whether the case has been reversed, distinguished, etc.).

The citator services put a *red symbol* (a flag for KeyCite, a box for BCite, and a stop sign for Shepards) next to a case to indicate that it is no longer valid, at least in part. Similarly, a red flag, box, or stop sign next to a statute or regulation indicates that it has been amended, repealed, or otherwise invalidated. You should not rely on any authority that has one of these red symbols next to it unless you are sure that it was only *partially* invalidated (for cases) or amended (for statutes and regulations), and that the part that was invalidated or amended does not affect your analysis.

The citator services put a *yellow or orange symbol* next to an authority to indicate that there has been *some* negative treatment (e.g., criticism from a court), even though the authority has not been invalidated. With regard to statutes and regulations, this often means that a pending bill or proposed rule may affect the statutory or regulatory provision. With regard to cases, it often means that a case has been *distinguished*, which may or may not be significant, depending on the facts. You should nevertheless review these distinguishing cases (particularly if they are in your jurisdiction) to see whether the distinctions they draw are relevant to your case or not. Likewise, before relying on a statute or regulation that has a yellow flag (or equivalent symbol) next to it, you should check the pending bill or proposed rule (simply click on the yellow flag to access it) in order to determine whether the proposed change would affect your reliance on the statute or regulation.

The most important thing to remember about using citators for validation is this: Before you turn in any work product, you should always use a citator to validate all the authorities you rely on in order to make sure that your analysis does not depend on an authority that is no longer valid.

Aside from validation, the other important purpose of citators is to *update* case research. To use this function, click on the *Citing References* link if you are using KeyCite, the *Citing Decisions* link if you are using Shepard's, or the *Citing Documents* link if you are using BCite. You can then use the various symbols the citators provide to obtain information about how the citing cases relate to the cited authority. The symbols tell you, for example, whether a citing case followed, criticized, or distinguished the cited authority. And they indicate how detailed the citing case's analysis of the point of law is.

The citators also list *headnote numbers* next to citing cases to let you know which points of law the citing cases discuss. This saves you time because it means you don't have to look at the citing cases that are not relevant to the point of law you are interested in. (However, if a citing case does not have a headnote number next to it, you will have to look at the case to determine which headnotes, if any, it discusses.) If, for example, you are only interested in knowing whether subsequent cases discuss the point of law summarized by Headnote 5 of a given case, you can narrow your review of citing cases to those that have a symbol for Headnote 5 next to the citation. (Alternatively, on WestlawNext, you can just click on the *Cases that cite this headnote* link below Headnote 5, which takes you directly to cases that have cited Headnote 5; you can do the same on Lexis Advance by clicking on the *Shepardize—Narrow by this Headnote* link below the headnote.)

In sum, citators are very important tools for legal research. You'll want to make sure you know how to use them, both for validating your authorities, and for updating your case research. (*See* Chapter 6, section J, for more on the importance of validating your authorities; *see* Chapter 4, section C, for more on using citators to update your case research.)

CHAPTER 9

PRIMARY SOURCES OF LAW

■ ■ ■

A. Constitutions

B. Statutes

C. Sources of Legislative History

D. Regulations

E. Cases

F. Court Rules

G. Local Law

H. Foreign Law and International Law

    1. Foreign Law

    2. International Law

I. Other Primary Authorities

Different types of legal documents carry, to varying degrees, the force of law. From municipal ordinances to the U.S. Constitution, lawyers rely on a variety of primary authorities to both analyze what the controlling law is and to persuade those vested with decision-making authority. This chapter discusses the principal types of primary authorities you are likely to rely on in solving legal research problems.

A. CONSTITUTIONS

Constitutions are the foundational documents of a legal system. In the United States, the U.S. Constitution is the highest legal authority in the land, though each state also has its own constitution to govern fundamental matters of state law. Constitutions are generally published within statutory compilations; a copy of the U.S. Constitution, for example, can be found in one of the volumes of the United States Code.

It is not likely that you will spend a lot of time on constitutional research in your practice, unless you happen to find yourself in a specialized field, such as media law or federal appellate litigation. In that event, you will probably come to rely heavily on specialized secondary materials, such as specialized practice manuals and loose-leaf services (*see* Chapter 8, sections B and F) to aid your research. But for the general researcher who only occasionally encounters a constitutional issue, constitutional-law research is largely a matter of case-law research, since the courts are charged with interpreting constitutional provisions, and most constitutional provisions, particularly at the federal level, have already been interpreted extensively by the courts. (Don't ignore secondary sources, however; these are very helpful in constitutional research, both for background information and for finding cases.)

If you are called upon to research a constitutional provision as part of a research project, probably the most efficient way to start your search for interpretive authorities is to review the case annotations for that provision in the annotated code where the constitution is published. First, of course, you would look for *controlling* cases on point. (With respect to the United States Constitution, that means cases from the U.S. Supreme Court and cases from the controlling circuit; with respect to state constitutions, it means appellate-court cases from the controlling state.) If you can't find any of those, then you would likely search for *persuasive cases.* If you are looking for persuasive cases interpreting the *U.S. Constitution,* you would normally look to U.S. Courts-of-Appeals decisions from the other circuits, then to U.S. District-Court decisions from within the controlling circuit, and then to U.S. District-Court decisions from the other circuits. You might also look to state-supreme-court cases that interpret the U.S. Constitution. If you are looking for persuasive cases to interpret a *state constitution,* you would look first to federal decisions within the controlling state. But if the operative language from the state's constitution tracks the U.S. Constitution, you can also look for guidance to other federal cases interpreting the equivalent provision in the U.S. Constitution. You could also look to appellate decisions from other states for guidance, if they construe similar language in their own constitutions, or to trial-court cases from the controlling state, if they are published. (For more on using non-controlling cases as persuasive authorities, *see* Chapter 7, section G.)

In some circumstances—where, for example, you can't find any controlling cases on point—you might want to research historical materials to interpret a constitutional provision. In interpreting a provision in the U.S. Constitution, for instance, you could look at historical records of the proceedings at the Constitutional Convention (*see, e.g.,* Max Farrand, *The Records of the Federal Convention of 1787),* and at the records of the subsequent state-ratification debates (*see, e.g.*, Merrill Jensen, *et al.*, *The Documentary History of the Ratification of the Constitution*).

You should probably talk with your supervisor before undertaking this type of historical research. But if you do decide to proceed with it, these types of compilations make a good place to begin your research efforts. Your reference librarian can help you locate them.

B. STATUTES

Statutes are the product of legislation. They begin as *bills* that their sponsors introduce in one or both legislative (or congressional) chambers. Once the bill passes both chambers and is signed by the governor or President (or the legislature overcomes an executive veto), the bill becomes a statute.

When a statute is first enacted by a legislature, it is published on its own as a *slip law.* It is then compiled chronologically with the other statutes that the legislature has enacted in a particular legislative session, and together these statutes are published as *session laws.* The session laws are subsequently incorporated into the jurisdiction's *statutory code,* which is a compilation of all statutes currently in force, organized by subject matter. If you have an issue of federal law, statutes are codified in the *United States Code*; if you have an issue of state law, statutes are codified in the applicable state code.

In most jurisdictions, the session laws constitute the official version of the legislation in the event there is any discrepancy between these various publications. (The federal session laws are published as the *United States Statutes at Large.*) The codes, however, being organized by subject matter rather than chronologically, are much more accessible for purposes of research. Accordingly, most lawyers use the annotated versions of codes (e.g., the *United States Code Annotated* or the *United States Code Service*) for their research, since these are updated more frequently than non-annotated versions, and they also contain helpful summaries of cases interpreting the statutes, as well as citations to secondary sources that are relevant to the statute.

Statutory interpretation frequently forms the centerpiece of a legal research problem. As long as a legislative enactment is not unconstitutional, it trumps other sources of law. Thus, except in those relatively uncommon circumstances when a court is called upon to determine the constitutionality of a statute, it is the court's job merely to interpret and apply the statutory language.

To be sure, judge-made law still dominates certain areas of state law, such as torts and contracts, where state legislatures have traditionally deferred to the common-law tradition. (There is no federal common-law tradition.) Accordingly, if you are researching a problem in one of these areas, there may not be a statute on point. But even in these areas of law traditionally left to the courts, legislatures in recent decades have shown an increasing willingness to become involved. So it is always a good idea to check whether there are any relevant statutes that might affect your legal analysis if you are uncertain whether decisional law controls. (*See* Chapter 3, section C(1), for a discussion of how to determine whether an area of law is controlled by legislation, and if so, how to go about finding the relevant statute(s).)

Once you locate a statute on point, you will then need to *expand* and *update* your statutory research to make sure (1) that you have located all relevant statutory provisions, and that the relevant statutory language is still current. This is a two-step process.

First, you should *expand* your research by checking whether there are any related statutory provisions in the code that might affect your analysis. Occasionally, related statutory provisions are codified in different parts of a code. To check for related statutory provisions, first review the sections preceding and following the relevant statutory section to determine whether they are also on point. Look also at the *editorial notes* for the statute to see whether there are any cross-references to other relevant provisions. (You can also use a citator to see whether there are any other statutory provisions that refer to the statute in question.) Then look at the *topical index* to see if there are other statutory sections listed under the relevant topic, and whether there are any related topics listed in the index. (It is also a good idea to check the code's table of contents to see whether any other sections of the code look like they might apply.) And finally, in order to ensure that you haven't missed any relevant provisions, it is helpful to run an electronic word-search of the entire code, using distinctive key terms from the relevant statute (e.g., from the statute's definition section) as your search terms.

The next step is to *update* your statutory research to ensure that the statutory language is still current. If you are researching online using one of the principal online commercial services, any recent changes to the statutory language will automatically be reflected, since these services are updated continually. If you are researching in print, however, updating takes a little work. You should start by reviewing the relevant pocket parts and supplements to see whether the statutory language has been modified since the permanent volume was published. Next, you should use a citator (Shepard's, BCite, or KeyCite) to make sure that the statute has not been more recently modified or repealed by the legislature, or stricken by a reviewing court. (*See* Chapter 8, section H(2), for more on using citators.) If the citator indicates that there have been very recent changes to the statutory language that are not reflected in the pocket parts and supplements to the code volumes, you will need to look at the jurisdiction's *session laws,* since statutes are published as session laws before they are codified. At the federal level, session laws (which are published as the *United States Statutes at Large*) can be found through various sources, including the *United States Code Congressional and Administrative News, HeinOnline,* and the United States Government Publishing Office's ("GPO's") free *FDsys* website (www.gpo.gov), as well as from the online commercial services.

Finally, whether you are researching online or in print, you should look at the editorial notes at the end of the statute. These will tell you, among other things, the dates of any significant amendments, and they will provide references to the relevant slip laws and session laws. This information is particularly important if you need to determine whether your particular research problem is governed by the current statutory language or some earlier version of the statute, and also whether a given case interpreting the statute is still valid or has been superseded by a change in the statutory language. (*See* Chapter 3, section C(1), for more on researching an earlier version of a statute.)

After you have expanded and updated your statutory research, you will next want to undertake further research regarding the proper *interpretation* of the statutory language. This requires you to look at additional primary sources, such as administrative regulations, interpretive case law, and perhaps also the statute's legislative history. These sources are discussed in the subsequent sections of this chapter. (For more on using these other primary sources as part of your statutory research, *see* Chapter 3, section C(1).)

C. SOURCES OF LEGISLATIVE HISTORY

A statute's *legislative history* consists principally of its stated purpose, the bills that gave rise to the final legislation, the statements of the bills' sponsors, the reports (and accompanying materials) of the committees that approved the bills, the records of committee hearings, the records of floor debates, and any executive signing statements. The legislative history serves as a tool for interpreting the meaning of statutory language. It is used to infer the legislature's *intent* as to the meaning of a statutory provision, particularly in situations where the language of the statute is unclear and there are no regulations or interpretive cases on point. Of the materials listed above, the *committee reports* are generally considered to be the most significant indicia of legislative intent.

Legislative history is not something you need to investigate every time your research problem involves a statute. Most of the time, the plain meaning of the statutory language and the case law (along with any applicable regulations promulgated under the statute) should be sufficient to guide your analysis. But in the appropriate context, legislative history can be an important (though somewhat controversial) tool, such as when the meaning or applicability of a statutory provision remains unclear even after you have carefully reviewed the statutory language and any available interpretive cases.

Putting together the legislative history of a statute is a two-step process. First, you should gather all the significant records that the legislature generated as a bill worked its way through the legislative process, including the relevant bill(s), committee reports, transcripts, etc. Then, you need to analyze these materials to determine whether they shed light on the legislature's intent. You should discuss with your supervisor whether it is worth pursuing the legislative history of a given statute before you start looking for these materials, since preparing a full legislative history can be fairly time-consuming if you have to start from scratch.

You should also check whether the materials have already been compiled into a "pre-packaged" legislative history before you undertake a full legislative history from scratch. Sometimes a case that interprets a statute, for example, will also analyze its legislative history. In that scenario, the court's interpretation of the legislative history is likely to be accorded significant weight by other courts, even if the case is not a controlling authority. Furthermore, even if the holding of the case is not directly relevant to your research, you can use the citations to quickly locate the relevant legislative-history materials.

In addition, you can often find commercially prepared legislative histories for certain statutes. The legislative histories for a number of federal statutes, for example, are catalogued in two well-known directories: Bernard D. Reams' *Federal Legislative Histories: An Annotated Bibliography and Index to Officially Published Sources*; and Nancy P. Johnson's *Sources of Compiled Legislative Histories*. These are available in most sizeable law libraries. WestlawNext and Lexis Advance have also compiled legislative histories on a number of statutes. And many loose-leaf services compile legislative histories for important statutes they discuss. Thus, if you are researching in a specialized area such as tax law, you can use the finding tables in a loose-leaf service, such as CCH's *Standard Federal Tax Reporter,* to find the legislative histories for a number of important provisions in the tax code. Finally, there are certain other commercial services that have compiled extensive collections of legislative histories, including *HeinOnline* and *Proquest Congressional.* Most sizeable law libraries carry subscriptions to these services; ask your librarian to help you locate them.

If you can't locate a pre-packaged legislative history, and you decide that finding the legislative history for a particular statute is nevertheless important to your research, then you will have to compile it yourself. For federal statutes, the most accessible source for a legislative-history overview is the *United States Code Congressional and Administrative News* ("U.S.C.C.A.N."). It is published by West Publishing and is available online as well as in print. U.S.C.C.A.N. does not provide complete legislative histories, but it often provides quite a bit of useful information about a statute, including its committee reports, which, as noted above, are generally considered the most significant of the legislative-history documents. U.S.C.C.A.N. also provides the important identifying numbers and dates for a statute and its earlier bills, which makes it easy to locate additional legislative-history materials.

If you need a more in-depth legislative history than you can obtain through U.S.C.C.A.N., the traditional gold-standard print resource is a publication called the *CIS Index.* The CIS Index provides finding aids and references to a variety of legislative-history materials, including committee reports, committee prints, hearing reports, and the original bills. It also provides references to the *Congressional Record,* which contains the floor debate for each bill. The CIS Index is now published by ProQuest. Thus, you can find an extensive collection of legislative history materials online via *ProQuest Congressional*, which is a subscription service that incorporates the CIS Index. Most sizeable law libraries carry subscriptions to it.

A number of legislative history materials are available on free websites as well. *Congress.gov* (www. congress.gov), for example, is a free government website that contains the texts of bills, committee reports, excerpts from the Congressional Record, and other information related to federal statutes. Another free government website that can be useful is the Government Publishing Office's *FDsys* website (www. gpo.gov), which contains many of the same documents, in addition to congressional hearings, congressional records, and presidential materials. The websites for the U.S. House (www.house.gov) and the U.S. Senate (www. senate.gov) also have links (click on *Legislative Activity* on the House site, *Legislation and Records* on the Senate site) through which you can access various legislative-history resources.

Finally, if you are struggling to put together a legislative history on a statute, don't forget about your friendly law librarian. A good reference librarian will have significant expertise on compiling legislative histories and can be a valuable resource in helping you find the necessary materials.

The above discussion has focused on *federal* legislative history. The documents that are germane to compiling a *state* legislative history are similar to those discussed above, and generally they are compiled in a similar manner. But many states do not publish everything that is important, and even when they do, finding the relevant materials is often more difficult. For that reason alone, it is less common for lawyers and judges to employ a legislative-history analysis in construing a state statute than it is for a federal statute.

Still, if you are diligent, legislative histories can often be compiled for state legislation. WestlawNext and Lexis Advance have compiled some basic legislative-history materials for most states, which can be helpful in getting you started on compiling a state legislative history. Another good option is to look in state-specific practice manuals, or in loose-leaf services. You can locate all the legislative-history materials available for any given state in William H. Manz's *Guide to State*

Legislation, Legislative History, and Administrative Materials, which should be available in your library. And finally, for free research, a good option is to try the websites of the individual state legislatures.

D. REGULATIONS

Regulations are rules generated by agencies to implement statutes. Often, Congress or a state legislature will authorize an agency to promulgate regulations in order to provide more complexity to a particular legislative scheme than Congress or the legislature wants to include in the statute itself. And while regulatory agencies are part of (and answer to) the executive branch of government, their rule-making authority derives strictly from a legislative delegation of power. Congress, for example, has authorized the Internal Revenue Service to generate a detailed regulatory scheme that expands upon the provisions of the U.S. tax code. Essentially, in this type of situation, the legislative body delegates limited authority to an agency to make law, subject to the ultimate approval of the legislature. Regulations flesh out the scope and applicability of a statute. But they cannot conflict with the statute or exceed the agency's legislative mandate, or else they are subject to being invalidated by the courts as exceeding their statutory authority.

Federal regulations are codified in the Code of Federal Regulations (i.e., the "C.F.R."). Like the U.S. Code, the C.F.R. is organized topically by titles, and then broken down further into individual parts and sections. However, newly promulgated federal regulations first appear in a government publication called the *Federal Register*, which contains the daily record of each agency's activities. Federal regulations are later codified in the C.F.R. when it is re-published every year. Both of these publications are available on the principal online commercial services, as well as in print. You can also access them on the Government Publishing Office's free *FDsys* website (www.gpo.gov). For purposes of regulatory research, the C.F.R. is the principal source you will want to use, though there are occasionally times when you may need to consult the Federal Register as well (e.g., to find the text of a proposed regulation).

The manner in which regulations at the *state* level are compiled varies by state. But most states tend to follow the federal system, publishing their regulations initially in registers similar to the Federal Register, and then codifying them later in administrative codes similar to the C.F.R. The principal online commercial services carry regulatory codes and registers for a majority of states, along with some other helpful state-specific administrative materials. Many loose-leaf services also contain updated compilations of state regulatory materials pertaining to particular specialties, along with relevant statutes, cases, secondary sources, and other materials. State-government websites are another good source for obtaining state administrative materials. Normally you can find these websites quite easily with a simple internet search, but if you are having trouble, you can consult the website of the National Association of Secretaries of State (www.administrativerules.org), which is a free resource that contains links to the relevant websites for all the states that have made their codes and registers available online.

Once you have located and reviewed one or more regulations that relate to your research problem, you will need to *expand* your regulatory research to ensure that you have found all relevant regulatory provisions. This is very similar to the process for expanding statutory research. You should start by reviewing the surrounding sections of the applicable administrative code to see if there are any other regulations that pertain to your subject. Then you should search the administrative code at large for other relevant regulations. The topical index and finding tables for the administrative code are helpful for this, as is the main table of contents at the beginning of the code. You can also use a citator to see whether there are any other regulatory provisions that refer to the regulation in question. And you can perform electronic word-searches online to find other regulations that might relate to your problem, using key terms from the regulatory provision you have already found, and from the definition section of the regulation, if there is one. Next, after having expanded your regulatory research, you need to *update* your research to ensure that the regulatory language is still current. If you are researching online with one of the principal commercial services, the updating process is automatic, as these services continually update the regulations. The Government Publishing Office's free *FDsys* website (www.gpo.gov) also publishes an unofficial version of the C.F.R., called the e-C.F.R., which is updated continuously. And loose-leaf services also update their contents on a regular basis.

But if you are not using one of these services, the updating process is a little more cumbersome. The traditional way to update federal regulations is by using a government publication called the *List of C.F.R. Sections Affected* (L.S.A.), which tells you, for any given regulation, whether it has been affected by any later agency action; if so, it directs you to the citation for the relevant Federal Register entry that affects the regulation. The L.S.A. is only published monthly, so you will also need to check the *Table of C.F.R Parts Affected*, which is found on the back of the most current issue of the Federal Register, to make sure that the regulation has not changed in the current month. If there have been any recent changes, the Table of C.F.R. Parts Affected will refer you to the relevant Federal Register cite(s) so that you can look at the changes.

The L.S.A. is available online as well as in print. The easiest way to access it is on the Government Publishing Office's *FDsys* website (www.gpo.gov), where it is listed under "Related Resources" when you click on the *Code of Federal Regulations* link. Remember that you can also access the online version of the Federal Register (which is published daily) on the *FDsys* website, as well as the online version of the C.F.R.

After you have expanded and updated your regulatory research, you will want to search for authorities that interpret the regulatory language. First, you will want to see whether there are any court cases that interpret the applicable regulatory language. Case law is important in construing the meaning of regulations, just as it is for statutes. (For more on finding cases that interpret regulations, *see* Chapter 3, section C(2).)

You will also want to look for any *administrative decisions* that might interpret the relevant regulation(s). Agencies have an adjudicative function as well as a rule-making function. Like courts, agencies conduct evidentiary hearings, called administrative hearings. These are less formal than court proceedings and are held before administrative law judges (i.e., "ALJ's") who work for the agency. And while these decisions are not binding like controlling court decisions, administrative decisions do nevertheless shed light on how an agency interprets its own regulations. Thus, they can be useful in predicting how an agency is likely to apply a regulation in future cases, and they can also be useful in persuading an agency that it should treat your client the same as a similarly situated party to a reported agency decision.

Agencies have their own internal appeals processes for administrative decisions. Normally, there are several steps to an appeal, and the secretary of each department has the final say. Furthermore, it is only when the agency's appeal process has been exhausted that the complaining party has a right of appeal to the courts.

To locate agency decisions, you can look at the relevant agency's website, or at a loose-leaf service that focuses on that particular area of regulatory law. Alternatively, the principal commercial services provide access to a number of agency decisions, both state and federal. On WestlawNext, for example, they are accessible from the main directory under *Administrative Decisions & Guidance.*

It can also sometimes be helpful, in construing a vague or ambiguous regulation, to see how similar language contained in other regulations in the administrative code has been construed. If, for example, a term you are interested in is defined elsewhere in the code with respect to another regulatory provision, you can look to that definition for guidance in interpreting the language of the regulation you are interested in. Likewise, if there is a court or administrative decision that interprets the term with respect to another regulation, you can use that interpretation as persuasive authority for interpreting the regulation that you are interested in.

Finally, if you want to do more in-depth regulatory research, you may want to look at other administrative materials (such as agency policy statements, agency manuals, general counsel letters, and advisory letters) that can shed light on the agency's own interpretation of the regulation. These types of materials are often published on agency websites. Some of them are available on the principal online commercial services as well.

You may also want to look at the history of the rule-making process by examining the text of a proposed rule, the public comments that were generated in response to the proposed rule, and any changes the agency made in response to the public comments. These materials too can (arguably) shed light on the meaning of specific provisions by revealing the reasons behind an agency's particular choice of words, similar to the way legislative-history materials can (arguably) shed light on the meaning of statutory provisions.

For federal administrative rules, proposed rules and the related public comments are published in the Federal Register and can be located through cross-references found in the final version of the rule that is published in the Federal Register. In addition, the federal government hosts a free website (www.regulations.gov) that is useful for finding comments, notices, ALJ decisions, and proposed rules. This website also allows users to readily submit their own online comments to proposed regulations.

E. CASES

When law students and beginning lawyers think of legal research, they normally have case research in mind. And indeed, case research is at the heart of most legal research projects. In areas of the law that are controlled by texts, such as a constitution, a statute, or an administrative regulation, judges play a key role in interpreting the meaning of the governing language, and so cases (i.e., judicial decisions) are crucial to researching these other primary sources. And in areas of the law that are still based on common law, judicial opinions themselves form the law. Thus, it is critical for the legal researcher to be skilled in finding and working with case law.

Judicial decisions are compiled in multi-volume print collections called *reporters*. Different courts publish their decisions in different reporters. United States Supreme Court opinions, for example, are published in three main reporters: the *U.S. Reports* (the official reporter), the *Supreme Court Reporter*, and the

United States Supreme Court Reports, Lawyers' Edition. Decisions from the United States courts of appeals are published in the *Federal Reporter.* And noteworthy decisions from the United States district courts are published in the *Federal Supplement.* Additional district-court decisions pertaining to federal procedural rules are compiled in the *Federal Rules Decisions.* There are also some lesser-known reporters published by commercial services that compile federal cases dealing with specialized areas of the law.

State-appellate-court decisions (most states do not publish trial-court decisions) are published in both the West Regional Reporter System and in official state reporters. The West Regional Reporter System divides the country into seven regions and compiles the various state appellate-court decisions for each of those regions (e.g., *North Western Reporter, South Eastern Reporter,* etc.). The official state reporters, on the other hand, compile appellate decisions by court. Colorado Supreme Court cases, for example, are published in the *Colorado Reporter,* while Colorado Court of Appeals cases are published in the *Colorado Court of Appeals Reporter.* The West regional reporter that covers Colorado (which is the *Pacific Reporter,* oddly enough) compiles cases from both of these courts, along with appellate decisions from Alaska, California, Hawaii, and all of the western states other than Texas.

The online commercial services carry all of the cases found in these reporters, and they generally make them available earlier than the cases become available in print. They also make available some cases that are not published in the official reporters, including certain state *trial-court* orders. You will need to check a jurisdiction's local rules, however, before citing a case that is not published in a reporter, since some courts limit or even prohibit their use. And even among courts that allow citations to unreported opinions, many hold that these opinions have persuasive force only.

Most appellate courts and some trial courts post their decisions on their own websites. These websites tend not to be updated as frequently as the commercial services, however, and they may not be as complete in their coverage. The websites also lack the comprehensive search capacity that the principal online commercial services offer. The same is true for the free online commercial services, such as *Findlaw* (www. findlaw.com) and *Justia* (www.justia.com), and for library websites, such as the Cornell Law School's *Legal Information Institute* website (www.law.cornell.edu). Your best bet for free case research may be *Google Scholar* (scholar.google.com), which is easy to use and has a robust search engine. Remember, however, that you will need to use a citator to verify the validity of cases you find on free websites.

Researching case law involves two principal tasks: finding relevant cases, and then expanding and updating one's case research. The task of finding relevant cases is discussed at length in Chapter 3, section C. The task of expanding and updating case research is discussed at length in Chapter 4.

Finally, there may be times when what you need to find is not a case itself (i.e., a judicial opinion), but rather some underlying filing in a case, such as a motion filed on a particular issue. For this, you will need to search the *court docket*. Docket information and case filings in federal cases are widely available on the United States Courts' *PACER* website (www.pacer.gov). They are also available on WestlawNext (click on *Dockets* in the main directory), Lexis Advance (*Browse → Sources → by Category → Dockets*), and Bloomberg Law (click *Dockets* on the main research menu). The commercial services also carry docket information and filings for a majority of the state courts. You can search for a given case by docket number, court, judge, case name, or keyword(s).

F. COURT RULES

Court rules govern the workings of courts. They concern the procedures that govern lawsuits, as well as more substantive rules, such as evidentiary standards and attorney disciplinary rules. At the federal level, the court rules you are most likely to research are the *Federal Rules of Civil Procedure* and the *Federal Rules of Evidence*. You might also need to look at the *Federal Rules of Criminal Procedure* or the *Federal Rules of Appellate Procedure*. State courts have similar compilations of court rules, which are often modeled after the federal rules. In addition, individual courts often have their own "local rules" that supplement the state or federal rules. Thus, any time you are litigating before a court, you should familiarize yourself with the general rules for the jurisdiction, as well as that particular court's local rules.

Finding court rules is relatively easy. One-volume compilations of the principal court rules for each jurisdiction are published by West Publishing, and are readily available. Most litigators have their own desk copies of the federal rules and of their individual state's rules. Free online access to the federal court rules is available at the *U.S. Courts'* website (www.uscourts. gov); just click on the *Federal Rulemaking* link. This site also has links to all the local rules of the various federal courts. Most state-court systems have similar websites that publish state-court rules online without charge. If you run an internet search for "[state] court rules," you can generally locate the desired site easily. Most such sites have addresses roughly similar to the *U.S. Courts'* website. New York's state-court website, for example, is located at www.nycourts.gov; Texas' website is located at www.txcourts.gov; Ohio's site is located at www.ohio

courts.gov; and so on. In addition, the principal online commercial services carry court rules for every jurisdiction.

As with other textual sources (e.g., constitutions, statutes, and regulations), court rules are subject to interpretation by the courts. Thus, if you have a research problem involving the interpretation of a particular court rule (e.g., whether a party opposing a motion for summary judgment under Rule 56 has raised sufficient evidence to defeat the motion for summary judgment), you will want to search for interpretive cases, starting with cases from the controlling jurisdiction. You can use the annotated version of the court rules for that jurisdiction to view summaries of cases interpreting the relevant rule; generally these annotated versions of court rules can be found within the jurisdiction's annotated statutory code. Cases interpreting court rules can also be located by using a case citator (*see* Chapter 8, section H(2)). Simply type the citation for the relevant court rule into the citator, just as you would for a statute, a case, or a regulation, and the citator will provide citations to all the cases and other materials that have cited that court rule. You can also run an electronic word-search online to find cases that interpret a particular court rule, using the citation for the rule as one of your search terms.

Keep in mind that if a state's court rules track the federal rules, as is usually the case, you can use federal cases interpreting a particular federal rule as persuasive authority for interpreting a parallel state rule. This can be very helpful when you cannot find any state cases on point. (For more on using persuasive authorities, *see* Chapter 7, section G.) Remember also to review the Advisory Notes and Amendments at the end of the annotated rule you are researching, as these too can shed light on the meaning of a rule.

Certain secondary sources are valuable for researching court rules. There are two large multi-volume treatises on the federal rules that are very well-respected: Wright & Miller's *Federal Practice and Procedure*, and *Moore's Federal Practice*. These treatises are often cited by the courts, so they can be useful as persuasive authorities as well in the appropriate case. In addition, many states have practice manuals devoted to their individual court rules. These are particularly helpful when a state's rules do not track the federal rules.

G. LOCAL LAW

Local law, also known as municipal law, involves the legal rules generated by cities, counties, towns, and villages. It can encompass a variety of subject matters, running the gamut from the relatively trivial (e.g., public park hours) to the complex (e.g., commercial zoning restrictions). Typical projects you might be asked to work on in this area include such things as liquor-license appeals, zoning appeals, housing-development applications, minor criminal violations, etc.

Municipalities derive their lawmaking power from the states in which they are situated, and they have only such powers as the state permits. Organizationally, their legal systems are similar to those of states. There is generally an organizational document called a *charter* that sets out the basic authority of the municipality. Typically, a municipal charter governs such functions as the election of city officials and council members, the administration of city departments (e.g., police, fire, parks), city budget issues and contracts, borrowing and taxing authority, and so on. Charters can also contain substantive provisions, however. In 1974, for example, the City of Ann Arbor, Michigan, became one of the first municipalities in the United States to decriminalize marijuana possession by making it a five-dollar (now

$25) civil infraction. This change took place when the city's voters approved an amendment to the city charter.

Most of the substantive provisions of municipal law, however, take effect not by virtue of charter amendments, but rather by virtue of *ordinances* passed by the city council. These ordinances are then codified into *municipal codes*, which, like other types of codes, are organized by subject matter. City charters also sometimes authorize certain municipal agencies (e.g., zoning boards) to promulgate *regulations* that flesh out the subject matter of the ordinances.

Municipalities are generally required to make these documents available to the public, though they may not all be published. Thus, if you are looking for the zoning regulations of a small village, you may have to pay a visit to the town hall. For all but the smallest municipalities, however, you should be able to find at least the charter and the municipal code online. Many of them are published and hosted on websites by commercial services such as *Municode* (www.municode.com), which makes available for free the municipal codes of over 3,000 municipalities around the United States.

If you can't find a municipal code there, try the municipality's website. Usually you can find that with a simple Google search such as "[city] municipal code"; if not, a free website called *State and Local Government on the Net* (www.statelocalgov.net) provides links to the websites of numerous municipalities and counties. The principal online commercial services also make municipal materials available online, including a variety of codes, regulations, and court decisions, as well as some secondary materials. WestlawNext, for example, carries Eugene McQuillan's *The Law of Municipal Corporations* (select *Practice Areas → Municipal Law → Secondary Sources*), which is arguably the leading treatise on the subject.

Once you have found the applicable municipal code, you will need to analyze the language of the applicable ordinance or regulation carefully, just as you would for a statute or regulation. You also want to see whether there is any decisional law or any other authority that sheds light on the meaning of the language. (For more on that process, *see* Chapter 3, section C(4).)

H. FOREIGN LAW AND INTERNATIONAL LAW

Because of their difficulty, foreign law and international law are topics generally reserved for an advanced legal research course, rather than a 1L course, so you are not likely to be assigned research projects in these areas as a beginning researcher. Still, given the increasing significance of globalization for the U.S. economy and for the practice of law in the United States, a basic familiarity with these topics is important. Accordingly, this section of the book provides a brief overview. (For a more detailed summary, *see* Kent C. Olson's *Principles of Legal Research*, or one of the several books devoted specifically to research in these areas of law, such as *International Legal Research in a Nutshell*, by Marci B. Hoffman and Robert C. Berring.)

1. FOREIGN LAW

"Foreign law" refers to the law of other (non-U.S.) countries. Even though you may never practice law abroad, there may be times when you need to have a basic understanding of another country's legal system and law. If, for example, your law firm represents a client that does extensive business in one or more other countries, it pays to have a basic understanding of the law in those countries—not so that you can practice law there, but just to be able to advise your client intelligently, and to be able to work more effectively with local counsel in those countries.

As a starting point for researching foreign law, keep in mind that there are two main types of legal systems in the world: (1) civil law, and (2) common law. (Note, however, that a small number of countries also rely to some extent on religious texts to guide their legal decisions.) In civil-law countries, statutory codes form the core of the legal system, and there is no common-law body of rules independent of the codes. Furthermore, unlike common-law systems, civil law systems do not put great weight on case law in interpreting the codes. Instead, they tend to rely more heavily on scholarly commentary as the principal guide to interpretation.

Secondary sources are very important for researching foreign law. Because different countries' legal systems differ somewhat in terms of their hierarchies of authority, you need a reliable guide to give you an overview of the law and to help you find and understand the significance of the various sources of law. A number of such guides are available, most of them focusing on individual countries. With regard to multi-country guides, the gold standard is probably the *Foreign Law Guide* (Marci Hoffman, ed.), which is available online by subscription from *Brill Online* (www.brillonline.com) under "Reference Works." This guide provides information on the legal systems of approximately 190 countries, including summary material as well as comprehensive outlines of the primary and secondary sources of law. Another helpful resource is the Yale Law Library's *Country by Country Guide to Foreign Law Research* (available at http://www. law.yale.edu/library/ → *Services* → *Foreign & International Research* → *Country by Country Guide*). This free service provides links to foreign-law materials available on the internet from a number of different sources.

The principal online commercial services also carry foreign law materials, including secondary sources.

WestlawNext, for example, has a significant collection of materials, including statutes, regulations, cases, secondary sources, and other materials. To access this collection, select the *International Materials* link in the main directory. (To access the collection on Bloomberg Law, select *Search and Browse → All Legal Content → Global Law*; on Lexis Advance, select *Browse → Topics → International Law* or *International Trade Law*).

Once you gain an overview of the country's legal system, and have identified the principal primary sources of law, then you can begin to search for authorities relevant to your particular problem. For the most part, that process is not all that different from what you are used to in researching American law: basically, you just follow the strategy outlined in this book. After you have reviewed secondary sources, you need to gather together all the primary sources that are relevant to your problem, and then analyze and organize your research results, keeping in mind that the hierarchies of authority vary somewhat between countries.

2. INTERNATIONAL LAW

International law refers to the legal rules governing the interactions between and among countries. Principally, these rules derive from *treaties* between countries, but that is not their only source. They also derive from *custom or practice*, *judicial decisions*, *scholarly writings*, and an amorphous set of so-called *"general principles of law."* Many practitioners of international law focus on international trade issues, particularly on behalf of large, multinational corporations. But other international lawyers work for a variety of other entities, including *intergovernmental organizations*, such as the United Nations, the European Union, or the World Trade Organization, and *nongovernmental organizations* (NGO's), such as Amnesty International or Human Rights First.

As with foreign law research, the use of a good guidebook or similar secondary source can make your life much easier when researching complicated issues of international law. There are several general encyclopedias that you can turn to for help; perhaps the best is the *Max Planck Encyclopedia of Public International Law*. As for guidebooks, the American Society of International Law's (ASIL's) *Electronic Resource Guide* (ERG) is a comprehensive online publication that serves as a guide to quality, up-to-date online resources covering important areas of international law. The ASIL also publishes a database called the *Electronic Information System for International Law*. This free online resource complements the ERG by organizing and providing links to web resources from the full spectrum of international law. Both publications are available at www.asil.org (select *eResources* from the *Resources/Pubs* drop-down menu).

Additionally, you may find some law journal articles and treatises that are helpful. The principal online commercial services carry extensive collections of both international journals and international treatises.

Once you have obtained background information on your research problem via guidebooks and other secondary sources, you can then move on to finding primary authorities (e.g., treaties) that will control your problem. The principal online commercial services carry decent collections of primary materials; many primary sources are also available from free online websites.

For example, a common research assignment for beginning researchers involves finding a treaty to which the United States is a party, verifying that it is still in force, and then analyzing the language of the treaty as it applies to the client's facts. (For more advanced projects, you may also need to find authorities that interpret the meaning of the applicable treaty language, and/or to examine the implementing legislation for the treaty.)

To locate the texts of treaties to which the United States is a party, the official source since 1945 has been a government publication called *Texts of International Agreements to Which the U.S. is a Party* (TIAS). The TIAS was originally a series of individual, consecutively numbered pamphlets that were later re-published in bound volumes, called *United States Treaties and Other International Agreements* (UST). The U.S. Department of State now publishes the TIAS on its free website (www.state.gov/s/l/treaty/). However, the online version only goes back to 1996. For information on finding older treaties, click on the *Finding Agreement Texts* link on the *Treaty Affairs* page of the website. You can also locate texts to U.S. treaties on the Library of Congress' free site (*see* www.congress.gov → *Resources* → *Thomas Site* → *Treaties*.)

Once you locate the treaty in question, you then need to verify that it is still in force. To do that, your best bet is to consult a U.S. State Department publication called *Treaties in Force* (available online at www.state.gov/s/l/treaty/). The print version is only published annually, but the online version of Treaties in Force is updated periodically throughout the year as needed on the Department's *Treaty Affairs* webpage. Treaties in Force is also available on WestlawNext.

If you're looking for treaties that involve countries other than the United States, your easiest option is the *United Nations Treaties Series* (treaties.un.org), which is a free website that carries all treaties registered with the United Nations by member countries since 1946.

I. OTHER PRIMARY AUTHORITIES

In addition to the primary sources discussed above, you may from time to time need to consult more obscure primary sources (and related types of materials) to find the answer to a legal research problem. This section discusses a few of the most significant ones.

Tribal law (also known as *Indian law* or *Native-American law*) is one such specialized source of primary authority that you should become familiar with. While much of this law derives from federal statutes, regulations, and case law, the individual sovereign tribes have their own legal systems as well, including their own constitutions, codes, and decisional law. The interplay between federal law pertaining to the tribes and the tribes' own laws creates a number of interesting and challenging legal issues.

A good amount of tribal-law material is available for free on the internet, although you may have to dig for it a bit. The websites of certain law school libraries have collections devoted to tribal-law resources. A good one is the *Native American Constitution and Law Digitization Project* (*see* www.law.ou.edu → *Law Library* → *Special Collections*), which is hosted on the University of Oklahoma College of Law's website. Similarly, the Tribal Law and Policy Institute has a helpful website called the *Tribal Court Clearinghouse* (www.tribal-institute.org), which can direct you to relevant primary authorities and other useful materials.

The principal online commercial services also carry fairly extensive collections of tribal-law materials. On WestlawNext, for example, click *Practice Areas*, then *Native American Law* to access these materials.

Another primary source that you may need to look at occasionally is the *executive order*. U.S. Presidents have long relied upon their inherent executive power to issue executive orders and proclamations (perhaps the most famous of which is the Emancipation Proclamation) in order to facilitate the administration of the executive branch, and this practice has become increasingly common in recent years. Governors of states have similar authority, though it tends to be more limited than presidential authority.

Should you need to look at an executive order or proclamation, federal executive orders are published first in the Federal Register and then in the C.F.R., in the same way administrative regulations are published (*see* section D of this chapter). In addition, U.S.C.C.A.N. includes important executive orders, along with legislative-history materials (*see* section C of this chapter). You can also access an extensive collection of presidential executive orders, along with many other useful presidential documents, at the American Presidency Project's free online website (www.presidency.ucsb.edu); simply click on the *Documents* link at the top of the page. As for state executive orders, you can generally access these on free state-government websites—often at the website for the governor's office. The principal online commercial services carry executive orders as well, both presidential and gubernatorial.

Finally, there may be times when you need to look at *public records* as part of a research problem. While not primary sources *per se*, certain public records are similar to primary sources in that they have significant legal effect.

The easiest way to access public records is via one of the principal online commercial services. WestlawNext, for example, has an extensive collection of public records, which are easily accessible from the main menus. These include death certificates, voter registration forms, UCC filings, corporate filings, deeds and other real property records, licenses, bankruptcy filings, criminal records, divorce records, etc. The only hitch is that some individual subscription plans do not include access to public records. WestlawNext's academic subscriptions, for example, do not include public records.

There are also a number of private online ventures that provide public records information for a fee (*see e.g.,* www.411.com). Unfortunately, however, there is no reliable, free site that serves as a comprehensive clearinghouse for all types of public records. So if you don't want to incur a fee, you'll have to look at various online sources, such as individual governmental websites. One of the most useful of these for business lawyers is the United States Security and Exchange Commission's *EDGAR* website (*see* www.sec.gov → *Filings*), which provides free access to more than 20 million company filings.

As always, if you are having difficulty finding a particular primary source, you should seek out the advice of a reference librarian. Reference librarians are a valuable resource, and they are there to help you.

RESEARCH STRATEGY CHECKLIST

■ ■ ■

Use this checklist after completing your research to ensure that you have appropriately followed the five steps set out in this book.

Step 1—Plan Your Research

❑ Did you formulate a precise *question(s) presented* and consider how it is distinct from related questions?

❑ Did you think about (and preferably make a list of) the principal issues you will need to address to answer the question presented, and the primary and secondary sources you plan to consult in your research?

❑ Did you use the question presented and your list of issues to generate effective *search terms*?

❑ Did you think about how to expand these search terms to cast a wider net?

❑ If you are researching online, did you think about how to combine the search terms into *electronic word-searches*?

Step 2—Consult Secondary Sources

❑ Did you review one or more secondary sources to obtain background information on your topic and to locate some initial primary authorities? If not, why not?

❑ After reviewing secondary sources, did you revisit your research plan and search terms to see if you can refine them?

Step 3—Conduct your Search for Primary Authorities

❑ Have you created a *preliminary outline* so that you can "link" the authorities you find with the various points in that outline?

❑ Did you consider which primary sources would be best to research first?

❑ Did you record the search terms and electronic word-searches you used to access the various sources?

❑ Did you consider using any alternatives to electronic word-searches to find authorities?

❑ If you did not find sufficient *controlling* cases on point, have you considered looking for *persuasive* authorities (e.g., cases from another state)?

❑ If you are planning to rely on a textual authority (e.g., a statute or a regulation), did you expand and update your research with respect to that authority?

❑ Did you record your research trail and your research results?

Step 4—Expand and Update Your Case Research

❑ Have you examined the citations within the cases you have already found to see whether they direct you to any other important authorities that you may have previously overlooked?

❑ Have you considered using the *West Key Number System* (or another subject-matter search) to find additional cases?

❑ Have you used a *citator* to update and validate your case research?

Step 5—Analyze and Organize Your Research Results

❑ Have you *pruned* away authorities that on closer inspection are not really on point?

❑ If you found multiple cases on the same point, have you thought about how to *prioritize* them for use in your final work product?

❑ If you found cases that appear to conflict, have you thought about how you might try to *harmonize* them?

❑ Have you prepared a helpful *short answer* to the question presented? If you cannot do so, have you considered what follow-up research you should undertake?

❑ Have you converted your preliminary outline to a *final outline* that sets out the issues you plan to address and "links" your final research results to those issues?

INDEX

References are to Pages

ADMINISTRATIVE DECISIONS,
177–178

ADMINISTRATIVE LAW
See Regulations, Regulatory
Research

**ADMINISTRATIVE MATERIALS,
MISC.,** 178–179

**AGE OF CASE, SIGNIFICANCE
OF,** 72, 133–134

AGENCY DECISIONS
See Administrative Decisions

***AMERICAN JURISPRUDENCE
2D (AM. JUR. 2D),*** 139

***AMERICAN LAW REPORTS
(A.L.R.'S),*** 145–146

***AMERICAN LAW SOURCES ON-
LINE,*** 90–91, 135

***AMERICAN PRESIDENCY
PROJECT,*** 192

**ANALYZING RESEARCH
RESULTS**
Generally, 70–79

ANNOTATIONS
A.L.R. annotations, 145–146
Annotated statutory codes, 42, 166–
167
In Digests, 155
In *Restatements,* 147
Proper use of case annotations, 98–99

ARGUING BY ANALOGY, 78–79,
115–116

**ARMSTRONG, J.D.S. & KNOTT,
CHRISTOPHER A.,** *WHERE
THE LAW IS: AN
INTRODUCTION TO
ADVANCED LEGAL
RESEARCH,* 135

ARTICLES, LAW REVIEW, 142–
144

**ATTORNEY GENERAL
OPINIONS,** 45

AUTHORITIES
Difficulty finding any authorities on
point, 113–117
Fear of missing authorities, 130–132
Finding too many irrelevant
authorities, 117–118
Persuasive
See Persuasive Authorities
Primary
See Primary Sources of Law
Secondary
See Secondary Sources of Law

BAR JOURNALS, 142–144

***BCITE,* ON BLOOMBERG LAW,**
65–67, 158–161

**BEGINNING RESEARCH,
DIFFICULTIES IN,** 106–108

BEST CASES, CHOOSING, 133–
134

**BILLING ARRANGEMENTS,
ELECTRONIC RESEARCH,**
90

BILL TRACKING, 46–47

BLOOMBERG LAW
See also Individual Sources of
Law
BCite, 158–161
BNA loose-leafs, 149
Dealmaker Documents and Clauses,
154
Draft Analyzer, 154
Outlines & Headnotes, 158
Practice Centers, 154
Research attorney assistance, 20–21
Topical searches, 158
Tutorials, online, 20–21

BOOK RESEARCH
See Library Research

BOOLEAN SEARCHES
See Terms-and-Connectors Searches

BRIEFS AND MOTIONS, SAMPLE, 152–153

BUSINESS INFORMATION, 155

CASE CITATORS
See Citators

CASE HIERARCHY, 75–77, 133–134

CASE SYNTHESIS, 73–75

CASEMAKER, 89

CASEMAP, **ON LEXIS ADVANCE,** 79

CASES
Generally, 179–182
See also Case-Law Research

CASE-LAW RESEARCH
Generally, 51–55
Expanding and updating case-law research, 62–65
Finding cases, 51–54
Harmonizing conflicting cases, 73–77
Hierarchy of authority, 75–77
Interpreting constitutions, 56–57, 164–166
Interpreting miscellaneous primary authorities, 55–59
Interpreting regulations, 47–51, 177–179
Interpreting statutes, 40–47
No cases on point, 113–117
Too many irrelevant cases, 117–118

C.C.H. MEDICARE AND MEDICAID GUIDE, 97–98

C.C.H. STANDARD FEDERAL TAX REPORTER, 171

CODE OF FEDERAL REGULATIONS (C.F.R.)
Generally, 174–177
C.F.R. Index and Finding Aids, 48
e-C.F.R., 176
List of CFR Sections Affected, 176
Locating regulations in, 48
Relation to *Federal Register*, 174–175
Table of C.F.R. Parts Affected, 176
West's Code of Federal Regulations General Index, 48

CHARTERS, MUNICIPAL
See Local Law

CHEETAH, 91

CIS INDEX, 172

CITATORS
Generally, 65–67, 158–161
BCite, on Bloomberg Law, 159–160
Expanding and updating case research, 65–67, 160–161
KeyCite, on WestlawNext, 159–160
Shepard's, on Lexis Advance, 158–160
Validating research results, 67, 103–104, 159–160

CODES
Administrative
See Regulations
Statutory
See Statutes

COMMERCIAL RESEARCH SERVICES, ON-LINE, 89–91

COMPUTER RESEARCH
See Electronic Research

CONFLICTING AUTHORITIES, HARMONIZING
See Harmonizing Research Results

CONFUSION IN RESEARCH, OVERCOMING, 119–121

CONGRESSIONAL RECORD, 172

CONSTITUTIONS
Generally, 164–166
See also Primary Sources of Law

CONSTITUTIONAL-LAW RESEARCH, 56–57, 164–166

CONTEXT OF RESEARCH, IMPORTANCE OF UNDERSTANDING, 25–28, 119–120

CORPUS JURIS SECUNDUM (C.J.S.), 139

COST CONSIDERATIONS, 87–92

COURTS, HIERARCHY
See Hierarchy of Authority

COUNTRY-BY-COUNTRY GUIDE TO FOREIGN LAW RESEARCH, 187

COURT DECISIONS
See Case-Law Research

COURT RULES
Generally, 182–184

CURRENT INDEX TO LEGAL PERIODICALS, 143

DEALMAKER DOCUMENTS AND CLAUSES, ON BLOOMBERG LAW, 154

DESCRIPTIVE WORD INDEX, DIGESTS, 52, 156–157

DIGESTS
Generally, 52, 155–158
American Digest System (West), 63
Descriptive Word Index (West), 52, 156–157
Finding cases with digests, 52–53,156–158
Key-number System (West), 52, 63–65, 156–158
On-line digest functionality, 52–53, 63–65, 156–158
Updating digests in print, 158
West Decennial Digests, 156
West Federal Practice Digest, 155–156
West General Digest, 156
West Regional Digests, 155

DOCKET SEARCHES, 181–182

DRAFT ANALYZER, ON BLOOMBERG LAW, 154

EDGAR (SEC), 193

ELECTRONIC INFORMATION SYSTEM FOR INTERNATIONAL LAW (ASIL), 189

ELECTRONIC RESEARCH
Generally
Advantages and disadvantages, 108–111
Cost considerations, 87–92
Electronic commercial research services, various, 89–91
Free websites, 90–91, 135–136, 181
Search filters, using, 39

ELECTRONIC RESOURCE GUIDE (ASIL), 189

ELECTRONIC WORD-SEARCHES
See also Search Terms
Broadening searches, 17–18, 113–117
Flexibility, importance of, 21
Generating, 15–21
Misuse of, 1, 6
Narrowing searches, 18–19, 117–118
Natural language, 15–16, 19–20
Potential downsides of, 20, 53–54
Terms and connectors, 16–19
To find persuasive authorities, 128

ENDING RESEARCH, KNOWING WHEN AND HOW, 128–130

EVALUATING RESEARCH RESULTS, 77–79

EXECUTIVE ORDERS, 191–192

EXPANDING AND UPDATING RESEARCH
Cases, 62–67
Other primary authorities, 68
Regulations, 174–179
Statutes, 166–169

EXTRAPOLATING, RULES FROM DISPARATE CASES, 73–77, 115–116

FARRAND, MAX, *THE RECORDS OF THE FEDERAL CONVENTION OF 1787,* 165

FASTCASE, 89

FDSYS WEBSITE (GPO), 46–48, 50, 135–136, 169, 173, 175–177

FEDERAL REGISTER, 174–175, 179

FEDERAL REPORTER
See Reporters

FEDERAL RULES
See Court Rules

FEDERAL RULES DECISIONS
See Court Reporters

FEDERAL SUPPLEMENT
See Court Reporters

FINAL WORK-PRODUCT, PREPARING, 79–80, 132–133

FINDING TOOLS
See Citators, Digests

FINDLAW, 91, 135

FOCUSING RESEARCH ON ANSWERS TO PROBLEMS, 99–100

FOLDERS, ONLINE, 95

FOREIGN LAW, 186–188

FOREIGN LAW GUIDE, 187

FORMS, *AM. JUR. 2D*, 152–153

FREE WEBSITES, 90–91, 135–136, 181

FULL-TEXT SEARCHES
See Electronic Word-Searches

"GESTALT" VIEW OF LAW, 28

**GOLF, AND RESEARCH
    STRATEGY,** 3–4

GOOGLE, 1, 185

GOOGLE SCHOLAR, 89–90, 114,
    181

**GOVERNMENT PUBLISHING
    OFFICE (GPO)**
See *FDsys* Website

GOVERNMENT WEBSITES
See Free Websites

GPO ACCESS
See *FDsys* Website

**HARMONIZING RESEARCH
    RESULTS,** 73–77

HEADNOTES
Expanding and updating case
    research, 62–67, 160–161
Not a substitute for reading cases,
    98–99

HEINONLINE, 144, 171

HIERARCHY OF AUTHORITY
See Case Hierarchy

HART, H.L.A., 115

**HOFFMAN, MARCI B. &
    BERRING, ROBERT C.,
    INTERNATIONAL LEGAL
    RESEARCH IN A
    NUTSHELL,** 186

HORNBOOKS, 150

*INDEX TO LEGAL PERIODICALS
    AND BOOKS,* 143

**INDEXES, USING SEARCH
    TERMS TO ACCESS,** 12–14

INDIAN LAW
See Tribal Law

INTERNATIONAL LAW, 188–190

JENSEN, MERRILL, *THE
    DOCUMENTARY HISTORY
    OF THE RATIFICATION OF
    THE CONSTITUTION,* 166

JOHNSON, NANCY P., *SOURCES
    OF COMPILED
    LEGISLATIVE HISTORIES,*
    171

JOURNALS, 142–144

JUDICIAL OPINIONS
See Case-Law Research

JURY INSTRUCTIONS, 151–152

JURY VERDICT REPORTERS,
    151–152

JUSTIA, 90, 135, 181

KEY NUMBERS, ON
    WESTLAWNEXT, 63–65, 127–
    128, 156–158

KEYCITE, ON WESTLAWNEXT,
    65–67, 158–161
See also Citators

**LAW LIBRARIANS,
    IMPORTANCE OF,** 92–94

LAW OF OTHER COUNTRIES
See Foreign Law

LAW REVIEWS, 142–144

LEGAL ENCYCLOPEDIAS, 138–
    140

*LEGAL INFORMATION
    INSTITUTE* (CORNELL
    LAW SCHOOL), 90, 135, 181

*LEGAL LOOSELEAFS:
    ELECTRONIC AND PRINT,*
    149

*LEGAL NEWSLETTERS:
    ELECTRONIC AND PRINT,*
    149–150

**LEGAL PAD, CARRYING IN THE
    OFFICE,** 84–85

LEGAL PERIODICALS, 142–144

LEGALTRAC, 143

LEGISLATION
See Statutory Research

LEGISLATIVE HISTORY
    Generally, 170–174
CIS Index, 172
Compiled legislative histories, 171–
    172
Congressional Record, 172–173
Definition of, 170
Federal, sources of, 172–173

HeinOnline, 171–172
ProQuest Congressional, 171–172
Purpose of, 170
State, sources of, 173–174
U.S.C.C.A.N., 172
Whether to pursue, 44, 170

LEXIS ADVANCE
    See also Individual Sources of
       Law
Advanced Search, 20
Browse Topics, 158
CaseMap, 79
Practice Advisor, 154
Research attorney assistance, 20–21
Shepard's function, 158–161
    See also Citators
Topical Searches, 52–53, 158
Tutorials, online, 20–21
Verdict & Settlement Analyzer, 152
Versus other commercial research
    services, 89–92

LEXISNEXIS CONGRESSIONAL
See *ProQuest Congressional*

LIBRARIANS
See Law Librarians

LIBRARY RESEARCH
Benefits of, 92–94
Versus electronic research, 108–111

**"LINKING," AUTHORITIES TO
    OUTLINE,** 11, 37–38, 79–80,
    95–96, 132

**LIST OF CFR SECTIONS
    AFFECTED,** 176

LOCAL LAW, 57–58, 184–186

LOISLAW, 89

LOOSE-LEAF SERVICES, 96–98,
    148–150

LOST
See Confusion in Research,
    Overcoming

**MANZ, WILLIAM H., *GUIDE TO
    STATE LEGISLATION,
    LEGISLATIVE HISTORY,
    AND ADMINISTRATIVE
    MATERIALS,*** 173–174

**MAX PLANCK ENCYCLOPEDIA
    OF PUBLIC
    INTERNATIONAL LAW,** 189

MCCORMICK ON EVIDENCE, 34

**MISSING AN AUTHORITY, FEAR
    OF,** 130–132

**MODEL CODES, USING AS
    PERSUASIVE AUTHORITY,**
    124

MOORE'S FEDERAL PRACTICE,
    27, 184

**MCQUILLAN, EUGENE, *THE
    LAW OF MUNICIPAL
    CORPORATIONS,*** 185

MULTIPLE CASES ON POINT
See Prioritizing Research Results

MUNICIPAL LAW
See Local Law

MUNICODE, 185

**NATIONAL ASSOCIATION OF
    SECRETARIES OF STATE,
    WEBSITE,** 175

**NATIVE AMERICAN
    CONSTITUTION AND LAW
    DIGITIZATION PROJECT,**
    191

NATIVE-AMERICAN LAW
See Tribal Law

**NATURAL LANGUAGE
    SEARCHES,** 15–16

NEWSLETTERS, 149–150

**NO CASES ON POINT, WHAT TO
    DO,** 113–117

NOTE-TAKING, 84–85, 95–96
See also Record-Keeping

NUTSHELLS, 150

**OLSON, KENT C., *PRINCIPLES
    OF LEGAL RESEARCH,*** 135

ORDINANCES, MUNICIPAL
See Local Law

**ORGANIZING RESEARCH
    RESULTS,** 79–80, 132–133

OUTLINES
Alternatives to linear outlines, 36
Converting to final work product, 80,
    132–133
Final outline, 79–80, 132–133
Preliminary outline, 36–38, 79, 132

PACER, 181

PERSISTENCE, IMPORTANCE
    OF, 100–102

PERSUASIVE AUTHORITIES
Definition of, 121–122
Finding, 127–128
Secondary sources as, 31–32, 126–
    127
When to use, 122–123
Which authorities to use, 123–127

PLANNING, IMPORTANCE OF, 6
See also Research Plan

POCKET PARTS
See Print Sources, Updating

PRACTICE ADVISOR, ON LEXIS
    ADVANCE, 154

PRACTICAL LAW, ON
    WESTLAWNEXT, 154

PRELIMNARY OUTLINE,
    PREPARING, 36–38

PRESIDENTIAL DOCUMENTS,
    191–192

PRIMARY SOURCES OF LAW
    Generally, 163–192
Cases, 179–182
    See also Case-Law Research
Choosing among, 72–73, 133–134
Constitutions, 56–57, 164–166
Court rules, 182–184
Definition of, 135
Legislative-history sources, 170–174
Local law, 57–59, 184–186
Miscellaneous other, 191–193
Regulations, 37–39, 174–179
Researching, generally, 40–59
Statutes, 40–47, 166–169

PRINT SOURCES
See Library Research

PRIORITIZING RESEARCH
    RESULTS, CASES, 72–73

PROCLAMATIONS,
    PRESIDENTIAL, 191–192

PROQUEST CONGRESSIONAL,
    171–172

PRUNING TANGENTIAL
    AUTHORITIES, FROM
    RESEARCH RESULTS, 70–
    71

PUBLIC RECORDS, 192–193

QUESTION PRESENTED
Formulating, 8–9, 28–29
Revisiting, 120–121

RAVEL LAW, 91

REAMS, BERNARD D., *FEDERAL
    LEGISLATIVE HISTORIES:
    AN ANNOTATED
    BIBLIOGRAPHY,* 171

RECORD-KEEPING,
    IMPORTANCE OF, 11

REDUNDANCY, IMPORTANCE
    OF, 131

REFERENCE LIBRARIANS
See Law Librarians

RE-FOCUSING RESEARCH,
    WHEN OFF TRACK, 33–34,
    119–121

REGIONAL DIGESTS, WEST
See Digests

REGULATIONS
Generally, 47–51, 174–179

REGULATORY RESEARCH
    Generally, 47–51
Agency decisions, 177–178
Administrative materials, misc., 178–
    179
C.F.R. Index and Finding Aids, 48
Code of Federal Regulations (C.F.R.),
    174–177
Enabling statutes, 48
Expanding and updating research,
    175–177
Federal Register, 174–175
Finding regulations, 47–51
Historical codes, 50–51
Interpreting regulations, 49–50, 177–
    179
Scope of rule-making authority, 48
State regulations, 175

REGULATORY LAW
See Regulations, Regulatory
    Research

REPORTERS, 179–180

RESEARCH PLAN, 6–12

RESEARCH
    QUESTION/PROBLEM
See Question Presented

RESEARCH STRATEGY,
    IMPORTANCE OF, 3–4

RESEARCH STRATEGY CHECKLIST, 195–197

RESEARCH TIPS
Generally, 83–104

RESTATEMENTS, 146–148

ROSS, 91

SEARCHES
See Electronic Word-Searches

SEARCH TERMS
See also Electronic Word-Searches
Combining into electronic word-searches, 15–20
Generating, 12–14
Importance of, 12
Modifying after reviewing secondary sources, 28–29
Using to access indexes, 12–14

SECONDARY SOURCES OF LAW
Generally, 137–161
A.L.R.'s, 145–146
As persuasive authorities, 31–32, 126–127
Definition of, 135
Importance of, 23–25
Legal encyclopedias, 138–140
Legal periodicals, 142–144
Loose-leaf services, 96–98, 148–150
Miscellaneous other, 150–155
Practice manuals, 140–142
Restatements, 146–148
To find primary authorities, 29–31
To obtain background information, 25–28
To refine search terms, 28–29
To re-focus research, 33–34
Treatises, 140–142

SESSION LAWS, 166–167

SHEPARDIZING AUTHORITIES
See Validating Authorities

SHEPARD'S, **ON LEXIS ADVANCE,** 65–67, 158–161
See also Citators

SHORT ANSWER, TO QUESTION PRESENTED, 77

SLIP LAWS, 166

SOCIAL SCIENCE RESEARCH NETWORK, 144

SOURCES OF LAW
See Primary Sources of Law, Secondary Sources of Law

SPECIALIZED RESEARCH MATERIALS, BENEFIT OF, 96–98

STARTING RESEARCH, DIFFICULTIES IN, 106–108

STATE AND LOCAL GOVERNMENT ON THE NET, 185

STATUTES
Generally, 40–47, 166–169
See also Statutory Research

STATUTORY RESEARCH
Generally, 40–47
And common law, 167
Attorney general opinions, 45
Bills, finding, 46–47
Expanding and updating research, 167–169
Finding statutes, 40–41
Historical codes, 45–46
Implementing regulations, 41–42
Interpreting statutes, 42–45
Persuasive authority, 42–45
Primacy of, 40, 167
Slip laws, 166
Session laws, 166
Statutory codes, 166–167
United States Code Annotated, 167
United States Code Service, 167
United States Statutes at Large, 166

STRING CITES, 72

SUPERVISOR, IMPORTANCE OF COMMUNICATING WITH, 85–87

SUPPLEMENTS, TO PRINT SOURCES
See Print Sources, Updating

SUPREME COURT REPORTER
See Reporters

TABLE OF C.F.R. PARTS AFFECTED, 176

TERMS-AND-CONNECTORS SEARCHES, 16–20

TEXTS OF INTERNATIONAL AGREEMENTS TO WHICH THE U.S. IS A PARTY (TIAS), 190

THOMAS **(LIBRARY OF CONGRESS SITE),** 190

TIME LOGS, 92

TIME, HOW MUCH TO SPEND ON RESEARCH, 111–113

TIPS
See Research Tips

TOO MANY IRRELEVANT CASES, WHAT TO DO, 117–118

TRANSACTIONAL RESEARCH, 154–155

TREATIES IN FORCE, 190

TREATIES
Generally, 189–190

TREATISES AND PRACTICE MANUALS, 140–142

TRIBAL COURT CLEARINGHOUSE, 191

TRIBAL LAW, 191

TROUBLE-SHOOTING GUIDE
Generally, 105–133

UNIFORM COMMERCIAL CODE (UCC), 125

U.S. STATE DEPARTMENT WEBSITE, 190

UNITED STATES CODE CONGRESSIONAL AND ADMINISTRATIVE NEWS (U.S.C.C.A.N.), 172

UNITED STATES TREATIES AND OTHER INTERNATIONAL AGREEMENTS (UST), 190

UNITED NATIONS TREATIES SERIES, 190

UNITED NATIONS WEBSITE, 190

UNITED STATES CODE ANNOTATED, 166–167

UNITED STATES CODE SERVICE, 166–167

UNITED STATES LAW WEEK, 149

UNITED STATES REPORTS
See Reporters

UNITED STATES SUPREME COURT REPORTS, LAWYERS EDITION
See Reporters

UNITED STATES STATUTES AT LARGE, 169

UNPUBLISHED OPINIONS, 180–181

UNSUCCESSFUL SEARCHES, WHAT TO DO, 113–117

UPDATING RESEARCH
See Expanding and Updating Research

VALIDATING AUTHORITIES
Importance of, 67, 103–104
Using a citator, 158–160

VERSUS LAW, 89

WEST PUBLISHING
American Digest System, 63
  See also Digests
Key Number System, 52, 63–65, 127–128, 156–157
National Reporter System, 63
Regional Reporter System, 180

WEST'S CODE OF FEDERAL REGULATIONS GENERAL INDEX, 48

WEST'S DECENNIAL DIGESTS, 156

WEST'S FEDERAL PRACTICE DIGEST, 155–156

WEST'S GENERAL DIGEST, 156

WESTLAWNEXT
  See also Individual Sources of Law
Advanced Search, 20
Case Evaluator, 152
CFR Index, 48
Descriptive Word Index, 52, 156–157
Digests, 155–158
KeyCite, 158–161
  See also Citators
Key Numbers, 63–65, 127–128, 156–157
  See also Digests
Practical Law, 154
Research attorney assistance, 20–21
Search filters, 39
Topical searches, 52–53, 127–128, 156–157
Tutorials, on-line, 20–21
Versus other commercial research services, 89–92

WOJCIK, MARK E., *ILLINOIS LEGAL RESEARCH,* 150

WORD SEARCHES
See Electronic Word-Searches

WORDS & PHRASES, 151

WORK PRODUCT, PREPARING
See Final Work Product, Preparing

WRIGHT & MILLER, *FEDERAL*
PRACTICE AND
PROCEDURE, 27, 30–31, 184

YAHOO, 1